TOEIC® L&R Test: On Target <Book 2>

<Revised Edition>

TOEIC® テスト：オン・ターゲット〈Book 2〉

［改訂版］

Rie Ooga
William J. Benfield
Ann N. Gleason
Terry L. Browning
David Thayne

NAN'UN-DO

TOEIC® L&R Test: On Target <Book 2>
<Revised Edition>

Copyright© 2019

by

Rie Ooga

William J. Benfield

Ann N. Gleason

Terry L. Browning

David Thayne

© 2019 All Rights Reserved

No part of this book may be reproduced in any form without written permission from the authors and Nan'un-do Co., Ltd.

TOEIC is a registered trademark of Educational Testing Service (ETS).
This publication is not endorsed or approved by ETS.

このテキストの音声を無料で視聴(ストリーミング)・ダウンロードできます。自習用音声としてご活用ください。
以下のサイトにアクセスしてテキスト番号で検索してください。

https://nanun-do.com テキスト番号 [**511948**]

※ 無線 LAN(WiFi)に接続してのご利用を推奨いたします。

※ 音声ダウンロードは Zip ファイルでの提供になります。
　お使いの機器によっては別途ソフトウェア(アプリケーション)の導入が必要となります。

※ TOEIC® L&R Test: On Target <Book 2>【Revised Edition】音声ダウンロードページは以下の QR コードからもご利用になれます。

はじめに

　TOEIC© L&R Test のスコア 750～800 点をできるだけ短期間で取得したい方達のためにこのテキストを書きました。著者は過去 20 年間 TOEIC 講座を主宰し、学期ごとに自分で教材を創ってきました。1 クラス(30 名)から始めた講座が 8 クラスになりましたが、それはひとえに学生の皆さんの TOEIC© L&R Test 得点数が伸びたからという事に尽きます。

　TOEIC© L&R Test でこれから 750～800 点以上を目指す方たちのために、私の講座で教えてきた数々の TOEIC© L&R Test に関する「最新の知識」「学習法」「テスト対策」をこのテキストに入れました。ですから、あなたはこのテキストを一冊学習し終えたら、実際に TOEIC© L&R Test を受験してください。前に受験したことのある人はきっと、かなり得点が上がっていることでしょう。しかし、初めて受けた人は予想したよりうまくいかなくて、がっかりするかもしれません。でも絶対にそこでやめてはいけません！

　TOEIC© L&R Test の特長の一つは大学入試のような一発勝負ではなく、何回でも受けられる、そして受けるべきだということです。私の講座でもあきらめずに 9 ヶ月、1 年と続けた学生は必ず 1 回ピョーンと得点がジャンプする（50～280 点）ことがありました。なにかロッククライミングのようにしがみついてガシガシ勉強し、何回目かのテストで、ジャーンと一つの峰に達するのです。ある日突然そうなることを楽しみに、何回もトライしましょう。

　TOEIC© L&R Test でいくら高得点をとっても、実際に英語が使えなければ何にもなりません。このテキストで学んで、実際の得点につなげるだけでなく、それをあなたの実力とするためには、リスニング部分を一度だけ学習してそれで良しとしては駄目です。何度も何度も shadowing* をしましょう。shadowing は「読み書きする英語」から、「聞いて話す英語」への飛躍を可能にする画期的な勉強法です。

　*shadowing については「**TOEIC の得点を上げ、英語を身につけるための学習法**」(p. 5) をご覧ください。

　TOEIC© L&R Test に使われている言語は米語ですが、Listening Section のナレーターは米国、英国、カナダ、オーストラリアの人たちが担当しています。いろいろな国のアクセントの違いを聞き慣れることが大切だからです。

　TOEIC© L&R Test は現存する英語能力テストの中で、一番ネイティブな英語が、日常的な表現とビジネスシチュエーションの中で使用されており、実用英語の勉強としても最適な内容です。ですから、TOEIC© L&R Test のための学習は同時に一番今日的な英語表現や語彙の学習になるということなのです。

　TOEIC© L&R Test では、文化的な背景に関する知識や専門用語に関するものは出題されませんが、やはり日常やビジネスに関する英語圏文化の理解が重要です。言語を学ぶということは、言語の背景にあるその国の文化を理解するということなのだと思います。ですから、TOEIC© L&R Test を何回か受験し、点数が 600 を超えたら、ぜひリュックを背負って、外国に出かけましょう。英語が少しでもできると、とても多くの国で現地の人たちとコミュニケーションをすることができるということをあなたは発見するでしょう。外国人の友人もできて、人生の幅も広がり、きっと英語を一生学習していこうという気持ちになることでしょう。そして「その気持ちを忘れずに学習を継続していって欲しい」というのが著者の心からの願いです。

　この本を創るにあたり、数々の複雑なプロセスを経ながら、専門的かつ教育的な立場から執筆してくださった私の大切な共著者たち、Ann Gleason, Bill Benfield, Terry Browning, David Thayne 諸氏に心から感謝します。また、南雲堂編集長加藤敦氏、校正者 Jim Knudsen 氏にとても貴重なご助言と大変なご尽力をいただきました。厚くお礼申し上げます。

著者　大賀リエ

TOEIC® L&R Test の問題形式

TOEIC は、「英語でのコミュニケーション能力」を見るテストです。マークシート方式の計 2 時間のテストで、Listening Section と Reading Section の 2 部に分かれています。テストは全て、統計処理されて、英語能力はどのテストでも、一定の能力を示します。

採点について

得点は、**Listening Section**（5〜495 点）、**Reading Section**（5〜495 点）、**TOTAL**（10〜990 点）のスコアが 5 点刻みで示されています。

LISTENING SECTION（所要時間 45 分） 100 問

リスニングテストでは、日常のまたビジネス関連を含む英語を聞いて、どの程度理解できるかが試されます。ビジネスの専門用語などは出題されませんが、会話のシチュエーションとしては、ビジネス関連を含むものが多いです。

CD は米国、英国、カナダ、オーストラリアの 4 カ国のナレーターでレコーディングされています。それぞれの発音の違いなどが慣れないと聞き取りにくいので、シャドーイングなどで練習して慣れておきましょう。

PART 1 Photographs 写真描写問題 6 問

1 枚の写真について 4 つの短文が 1 回だけ放送されます。一番写真と合っていると思われるものを (A) (B) (C) (D) から選びます。写真中の人物や風景、状景などが文として読まれます。文そのものは難しいものではなく、またほとんどの文は<u>現在形、現在進行形</u>、たまに<u>現在完了形</u>です。ただし、正解の他に、受験者を迷わせる文が入っているので、語彙の選択に気をつけること。Listening Section では一番得点しやすいパートです。

PART 2 Question-Response 応答問題 25 問

1 つの質問または文と、それに対する (A) (B) (C) 3 つの応答が 1 回だけ放送されます。設問も応答もテストブックにはプリントしてありませんから、ある意味では聞くことだけに集中できるパートです。日常生活やビジネスの場面で、<u>いかに的確に応答できるか</u>を試すパートです。<u>始めの疑問詞と質問のキーワード</u>を聞き逃さないようにしましょう。

PART 3 Conversations 会話問題 39 問

2 人またはそれ以上の人数による会話が 1 回だけ放送されます。時にそれに加えて、テストブックに図表などが出題されています。質問は 3 問です。正しいと思われるものを (A) (B) (C) (D) 4 つの選択肢から選びます。PART 2 と違い、質問も選択肢もテキストブックに印刷されていますから、まず<u>会話が始まる前に 3 つの質問をさっとスキャンしてキーワードを拾う</u>ようにしましょう。いかに日常生活、ビジネスの場面でのネイティブの表現が理解できるかが試されるパートです。

PART 4 Talks 説明文問題 30 問

説明文、指示文、伝言、スピーチなどのアナウンスメントがあり、1 回だけ放送されます。質問は 3 問です。1) 図表を見て答える、2) 説明文中の意味を問う質問などがあります。
正しいと思われるものを (A) (B) (C) (D) から選びます。Listening Section で最難関とされるパートです。質問も選択肢もテストブックに印刷されていますから、PART 3 と同じく<u>アナウンスメントが始まる前にまず質問のキーワードだけでもスキャンすること</u>が大切です。

READING SECTION（所要時間 75 分） 100 問

リーディングテストでは、日常的な、またビジネス上の表現に関する文が出題されます。3 つのパートの指示を読んで、<u>より多くの問題に解答すること</u>が重要です。

PART 5 Incomplete Sentences 短文穴埋め問題 30 問

語彙と文法に関する問題が出題されます。文中の空欄に適当と思われる語を (A) (B) (C) (D) から選びます。短時間で 30 問こなさなければなりませんから、<u>1 つの問題に留まらないこと</u>。1 問 20 〜 30 秒程度で解答していくよう練習しましょう。

PART 6 Text Completion 長文穴埋め問題 16 問

語彙、イディオム、文の理解に関する出題で、記事、手紙、メモなどの文章の中に 4 つのブランクがあり、それぞれ (A) (B) (C) (D) から正しいと思われる答えを選びます。4 題中、1 題は文をそのまま当てはめる問題で、文脈の理解を見るテストです。<u>宛名、差出人、用件の項を読み、ブランクの前後を読んで解答していきましょう。</u>

PART 7 Reading Comprehension 読解問題 54 問

Single passages　　　一つの文書　29 問
Multiple passages　　複数の文書　25 問

Reading Section で最難関のパートです。インスタントメッセージ、手紙、新聞記事、公文書、オフィスメモ、E メール、広告、指示文などの文章を読んで (A) (B) (C) (D) から正しいと思われる答えを選びます。また、1 つだけでなく、3 つの関連する文書に関する設問があります。膨大な語彙とたくさんの長文を短時間でこなすためには、まず質問を読んで、その答えになるキーワードを本文中でスキャンして見つけることです。日頃から、スキャニングの練習をみっちりしておくことが高得点につながります。

TOEIC の得点を上げ、英語を身につけるための学習

LISTENING SECTION: Shadowing（シャドーイング）の仕方を身につけよう

Shadowing（シャドーイング）とはレコーディングされた教材をかけっぱなしにして、ほんのちょっと遅れて声を出しながらついて行く方法です。ネイティブの英語について、何回も練習するうちに自然に発音、イントネーション、言葉の意味が身につくようになります。次の方法に従ってください。

- STEP 1　TOEIC 用の自分にあった参考書を書店で見つけ問題を解く。しかしそれだけでもう忘れてしまうのでなく、ここから本当の勉強が始まるのです。
- STEP 2　CD をスタート。トランスクリプトを見ながら、一緒に声を出して練習する。
- STEP 3　1 つの Unit または 1 つの PART を、数回繰り返してください。できるだけしっかり声を出して読みましょう。ついていけないところは「ウーウー」と声を出しているだけでも良いから、PART の終わりまで続ける。<u>絶対に途中で CD をとめないこと。</u>
- STEP 4　<u>テキストを見なくても CD についていけるまで練習しましょう。</u>

声を出せない電車の中でも、この方法で、口の中で shadowing しながら練習することができます。毎日続けて練習すること。不思議ですが、そうするとある日突然と言ってよいくらい英語が耳に入ってくるようになります。

READING SECTION: Scanning（スキャニング）しながらキーワードを把握する練習をしよう

Reading Section 得点のための最大の武器は scanning（スキャニング）です。スキャニングとは電話帳や辞書から必要な情報だけを読み取るように、質問に対するキーワードを本文から読み取ることです。

また TOEIC 受験経験の少ない人は、自習用テキストとしては、比較的易しい英語からなる TOEIC© Bridge の問題集を使って学習しても良いでしょう。まずここで大切なのはタイマーを使って、決められた時間内にスキャンしながら解答する練習をすることです。

STEP 1	Reading Section の一つの PART を選び全体の時間から、その問題にかけるべき時間を割り出す。
STEP 2	タイマーを設定して、問題に取り組む。だらだらと長時間かけて辞書を引きながらでは、実力になりません。必ずタイマーを設定してから始めること。
STEP 3	長文は、1) まず問題を読む　2) 本文をスキャンして答えになるべきキーワードを見つけ、斜線でチェック（／）する。
STEP 4	解答をチェックし、その後、しっかり辞書を引いたりしながらもう一度読む。

また、インターネットで、自分の興味のある分野を英語で検索し、ダウンロードして読みましょう。必ず 1 日 1 回 1 つの記事を読む習慣をつけましょう。そのときも、1) タイマーを設定し、2) キーワードをチェックしながら読んでください。速読の習慣を身につけることが大切です。

Review Test について

Review Test 1, 2 のスコアシートが巻末についています。間違った問題を確認し、満点になるように練習しましょう。

Contents

Unit 1   Travel — 10

Unit 2   Health — 20

Unit 3   Entertainment — 29

Unit 4   Going House Hunting — 38

Unit 5   Ecology — 47

Review Test 1 (Units 1-5) — 57

Unit 6   Careers and Employment — 69

Unit 7   Advertisements and Sales Campaign — 79

Unit 8   Communications — 88

Unit 9   Complaints and Troubleshooting — 98

Unit 10   Innovations and Technology — 108

Review Test 2 (Units 6-10) — 118

Review Test 1, 2   Answer Sheet — 129

Grammar Points

Unit 1　**Word Forms**　語形に関する問題

Unit 2　**Tricky Prepositions**　前置詞

Unit 3　**Essential Comparatives**　大切な比較表現のいろいろ

Unit 4　**Articles and Quantifiers**　冠詞と数量詞

Unit 5　**Participles**　分詞構文 ~ing と ~ed

Unit 6　**Future Tense**　未来形のさまざまな表現

Unit 7　**Subject-Verb Agreement**　主語と動詞の関係

Unit 8　**TO+Verb vs Verb+ING**　TO をとる動詞と ING をとる動詞

Unit 9　**Past Modals with "have"**　過去完了形の文

Unit 10　**Conditional Sentences**　条件文（仮定法）

Unit 1
Travel

Key Expressions

Step 1 A 欄の語彙に合う訳を B 欄から選びましょう。

A.
1. metal detector
2. good luck charm
3. nuisance
4. hold up
5. set off
6. deposit (v)
7. get away
8. personal belongings

B.
a. 停滞させる
b. 遠出する
c. お守り
d. （物を所定の場所に）置く
e. 金属探知機
f. 所持品；身の回り品
g. 厄介なこと
h. 鳴らす

Dialog: At Airport Security

Step 2 Dialog の中の空白に Key Expressions から当てはまる言葉を選びましょう。必要ならば語形を変えて入れてください。

Teri and Don are waiting in line at Airport Security.

Teri: Will you look at how long this line is? We'll never get through security in time to catch our flight. We should have gotten to the airport earlier.

Don: Well, it is summer vacation, and we are flying during peak season. I suppose everyone must be trying to (A) (　　　　).

Teri: I just hope we don't have to take our shoes off again. That was such a (B) (　　　　) last time, and it really (C) (　　　　) the line.

Security: Good morning, ma'am. You can sit here to take your shoes off, and please (D) (　　　　) your handbag, belt, and hair clip in this tray, along with your other (E) (　　　　).

Teri: Oh, no. Not my hair clip. Now my hair will fall in my face.

Security: I'm sorry, ma'am, but your hair clip has metal in it, and that will (F) (　　　　) the (G) (　　　　). Please go on through. Now you, sir.

(a buzzer sounds)

Don: What's that noise?

Security: Do you have any metal in your pockets, sir? Coins or anything like that?

Don: Just my (H) (　　　　). I always carry it with me when I travel.

Security: Go back through and place it in the tray and then come through the detector again. Next time, you two should read the TSA Pre-Check pamphlet. That way, you can avoid a lot of hassle for you and me!

Dialog Comprehension

Step 3　Dialog に関する次の質問に答えましょう。

1. What caused the metal detector to make a buzzing sound?
   (A) The coins in the woman's handbag
   (B) The metal in the woman's hair clip
   (C) The good luck charm in the man's pocket

2. What does the man at Security suggest to the man and the woman?
   (A) That they read the Pre-Check pamphlet.
   (B) That they arrive at the airport earlier.
   (C) That they stop traveling so often.

LISTENING SECTION

PART 1 Photographs （写真描写問題）（2問）

文を聞いて写真と一番一致するものを (A) (B) (C) (D) から選びなさい。

1. (A) (B) (C) (D)

2. (A) (B) (C) (D)

PART 2 Question-Response （応答問題）（3問）

質問または文を聞いて、一番適当と思われる応答を (A) (B) (C) から選びなさい。

1. (A) (B) (C)   2. (A) (B) (C)   3. (A) (B) (C)

PART 3 Conversation （会話問題）（3問）

会話文を聞いて質問に対する一番適当と思われる答えを (A) (B) (C) (D) から選びなさい。

Hotel Type of Room	Price
Valencia Double	$350
Alhambra Single	$250
Red Rooster Inn Family	$350
Best Stay Double	$300
Chateau Suite	$400

1. Which of the following do the man and the woman want their vacation hotel to have?
   (A) A good website
   (B) The lowest possible price
   (C) Different kinds of rooms
   (D) A swimming pool

2. Look at the graphic. If the man is looking for a double room, which hotels should he look at?
   (A) The Valencia and the Red Rooster Inn
   (B) The Alhambra and the Valencia
   (C) The Valencia and the Best Stay
   (D) The Best Stay and the Chateau

3. Why is the man confused?
   (A) There are so many websites.
   (B) There is a big difference in prices among the advertised hotels.
   (C) He can't find the Valencia hotel on the website.
   (D) He can't find a double room at the business traveler's rate.

Unit 1

PART 4 Talks （説明文問題）（3問）

次のアナウンスメントを聞いて、質問に対する一番適当と思われる答を (A) (B) (C) (D) から選びなさい。

1. Where is the activity taking place?
   (A) At a zoo
   (B) In a forest
   (C) In a wetlands preserve
   (D) In a flower garden

2. What does the speaker say will be especially interesting about today's hike?
   (A) the swampy ground
   (B) the plant life
   (C) the zebras
   (D) a certain variety of butterfly

3. What are hikers advised to do?
   (A) Wear sunscreen
   (B) Pay the small charge for the hike
   (C) Stay off the grass
   (D) Pay close attention to the speaker

PART 1 Photographs 写真描写問題
PART 1 出題形式

実際のテストは6問あります。
人物または物、風景などについて、それぞれ4つの文が読まれます。一番正確に写真を描写していると思われる文を選びましょう。

TOEICのための満点アプリ
PART 1 Photographs

Directions が読まれている間にしっかり、写真を見ておきましょう。
写真のテーマは大多数が「人物」で、あとは「風景、物の位置関係に関して」です。また、問題文の時制は現在進行形 The woman is giving a speech.（女性はスピーチをしている。）または現在形 The woman seems to be the chairperson.（女性は議長だと思われる。）です。稀に現在完了形 The bed has been made.（ベッドは整頓されている。）などトリッキーな表現が出題されます。

READING SECTION

Grammar Points
TOEIC 頻出ポイント：Word Forms　語形に関する問題

英語で自分の意志を正しく相手に伝えるためには、適切な語彙を正しい形で使うことが大切です。TOEIC PART 5 と PART 6 では語形の問題が頻出ポイントです。基本語彙と一緒に変化した形を覚えましょう。

▶ **Point 1**　一つの基に接頭語や接尾語を付けて多くの派生語ができます。

動詞	名詞	人名詞	形容詞	否定の形容詞
employ	employment	employee	**employed**	**un**employ**ed**

▶ **Point 2**　動詞に -ion, -ation などを加えることで名詞（主に抽象名詞）になります。

動詞	名詞	動詞	名詞	動詞	名詞
preserve →	preserv**ation**	decide →	decis**ion**	inform →	inform**ation**

▶ **Point 3**　動詞に -ive or -ative などを加えると形容詞になります。

動詞	形容詞	動詞	形容詞	動詞	形容詞
preserve →	preserv**ative**	decide →	decis**ive**	inform →	inform**ative**

▶ **Point 4**　-ics で終わる名詞の形容詞形（または副詞形）と人を表す名詞は次のように変化します。

名詞	形容詞（副詞）	人名詞
mathemat**ics** →	mathematical(ly) →	mathematician
polit**ics** →	political(ly) →	politician
tact**ics** →	tactical(ly) →	tactician

Grammar Quiz (5問)

次の文を読んで、一番適当と思われる語を選びなさい。

1. The high school's new program will include more courses related to STEM—that is Science, -------, Engineering and Math.
   (A) Technological
   (B) Technical
   (C) Technology
   (D) Technique

2. Please make sure that all the trays and overhead bins are ------- before take-off.
   (A) secure
   (B) safe
   (C) security
   (D) safety

3. At airport security, all passengers have to go through the metal -------.
   (A) detecting
   (B) detector
   (C) detective
   (D) detectable

4. Dave and Jan have decided to move to a larger city so that they can enjoy more ------- events.
   (A) culturally
   (B) cultured
   (C) cultural
   (D) culture

5. Please ------- immediately to the boarding gate.
   (A) proceed
   (B) proceeding
   (C) procession
   (D) process

PART 5 Incomplete Sentences （短文穴埋め問題）（2問）

次の文の空欄に一番適当と思われる答を (A) (B) (C) (D) から選びなさい。

1. A special section of the national park has been set aside for the ------- of an endangered owl that makes it home in the park.
   (A) preservance
   (B) preservability
   (C) preserved
   (D) preservation

2. The latest statistics clearly show that ------- figures are moving up.
   (A) employment
   (B) employed
   (C) employer
   (D) employee

PART 6 Text Completion （長文穴埋め問題）（4問）

次の文の4つの空欄に一番適当と思われる答を (A) (B) (C) (D) から選びなさい。

Text: Article

When you have a great idea, what is the best way to present it to the public? One exciting new way to do this is TED Talks, short speeches or presentation on a variety of subjects that are recorded on video and uploaded to the Internet where anyone can ------- them for free. The talks are sponsored by the nonprofit TED Foundation, whose goal is to encourage the spread of ideas and to provide a platform for people to think about and discuss today's most important issues. TED also holds ------- where ------- can view TED Talks and learn how to make their own. Recent topics have dealt with body language, psychology, how to motivate employees, the key to happiness, and the nuisance of spam email. TED also awards a TED Prize annually for an idea that encourages global change. This year's prize was awarded to a proposal for a program that will bring comprehensive medical care to remote areas of the world. -------.

1. (A) accesible
   (B) entrance
   (C) accession
   (D) access

2. (A) conferences
   (B) conferees
   (C) confer
   (D) contests

3. (A) attentions
   (B) attendants
   (C) attentives
   (D) attendees

4. (A) TED Talks will no longer be available on the Internet due to financial problems.
   (B) The TED Foundation expects to make a large profit from its talks.
   (C) The plan would send to the areas doctors and nurses who would not only offer medical care but would also provide medical training.
   (D) The TED prize will not be awarded after all this year because of a lack of good ideas.

TOEICのための満点アプリ
PART 6 Text Completion 長文穴埋め問題

TOEIC PART 6は4つのパッセージ出題され、各パッセージに4問の空白があります。PART 5との大きな違いはかたや短文、こちらは長文で、文脈を考えることも必要な出題であるという点です。

▶ **各パッセージの長さは 12-18 行**

各パッセージの長さは12-18行程度で、4箇所の空白部分があり、それを (A) (B) (C) (D) から選んで埋めていきます。

▶ **1問を 20-30 秒以内で解答する**

READING SECTIONは全部で75分ですが、PART 5で12-14分すでに費やしているので、1) パッセージをどういう種類の文章かを見るために、ざっと skimming スキミングする、そして 2) 1問を20-30秒程度で解くことが必要です。skimmingの時間も含め PART 6 全部で12問を8-10分で終わるようにしましょう。

Unit 1

PART 7 Reading Comprehension (読解問題)（5問）

次の3つの文書を読んで、一番適当と思われる答を (A) (B) (C) (D) から選びなさい。

Material 1:

E-mail 1
From: John White
To: Sam@TravelFixIt.com
Date: August 10
Subject: Compensation
Dear Sam: I hope you can help me with this problem. My wife and I flew on Stateside Airlines from Chicago to the Bahamas, with a change in Atlanta. We were "bumped" from our connecting Econo Airlines flight in Atlanta and had to spend the night there. Shouldn't Econo compensate us for our overnight expenses? After all, it was the airline that denied us boarding. I thought there were rules covering this kind of situation. Is the airline just being cheap? Or are we not eligible for some reason? We spent over $300 on the hotel and meals. "Bumped" in Atlanta. John White Purchasing Manager

Material 2:

E-mail 2
From: Sam@TravelFixIt.com
To: customerservice@EconoAir.com
Date: August 11
Subject: Compensation
To Customer Service: I would like to bring to your attention the case of Mr. and Mrs. John White, who were removed from your flight #723 from Atlanta to the Bahamas on July 31st. They believe they were involuntarily denied boarding and, as a result, were obliged to spend over $300 of their own money on overnight accommodations. Under government regulations, they should be entitled to compensation for their expenses as well as for the delay. Kindly look into this matter and give it your prompt attention. Sincerely, Sam

Material 3:

E-mail 3
From: Sam@TravelFixIt.com
To: John White
Date: August 20
Subject: Compensation
Dear Mr. White:
I contacted Econo Air in regards to your case. According to the airline, your initial stateside flight from Chicago was delayed, which meant that you were not on time for your connection. In other words, the airline claims that you were not actually "bumped" from your flight, and that they are not under any legal obligation to compensate you. However, since they want to maintain good customer relations, they are offering you a choice of 20,000 frequent-flier miles or a $200 travel voucher. Hope this helps, Sam

1. Why is Mr. White contacting Sam@TravelFixIt.com?
   (A) He believes that he and his wife were unfairly kept off a flight.
   (B) He and his wife changed their travel plans.
   (C) He and his wife were put on the wrong flight.
   (D) The airline lost his and his wife's reservations.

2. What does Mr. White want Sam to do for him?
   (A) He wants a full refund on his ticket.
   (B) He wants to be compensated for a cancelled flight.
   (C) He wants to be compensated for a hotel stay.
   (D) He wants Sam to pay him $300.

3. What are the government regulations related to Mr. White's situation?
   (A) The regulations say that the Whites are entitled to full compensation.
   (B) The regulations say that the Whites are not entitled to compensation.
   (C) The regulations say that the Whites are entitled to compensation for the hotel but not the meals.
   (D) This situation is not covered by any government regulations.

4. How does Sam respond to Mr. White's request?
   (A) He refuses to offer any help.
   (B) He can't help because he doesn't think the airline was at fault.
   (C) He is too busy to give attention to the Whites' problem.
   (D) He agrees to do what he can for Mr. White.

5. How is the situation resolved?
   (A) Mr. and Mrs. White can now board their flight.
   (B) Mr. and Mrs. White will be offered a choice of compensations.
   (C) Mr. and Mrs. White will receive a check for $300.
   (D) The airline will not do anything at all for them.

TOEIC のための満点アプリ
PART 7 Reading Comprehensiond 読解問題

▶ NOT を含む質問
PART 7 にはいくつか次のような NOT を含む質問があります。NOT は大文字で強調してあります。文中にその情報が無いことを確認していかなければならないので、かなり時間をとります。
例：In this passage, what is **NOT** mentioned as a treatment for a cold?
（このパッセージで風邪の治療法として触れていないのはどれですか？）

▶ 語彙の意味を問う質問
PART 7 で必ず出題されるものに語彙の意味を問う設問があります。パターンは2つ：
Pattern 1. Which expression is closest in meaning to "take advantage of" in line xx?
（xx 行目、"take advantage of（うまく利用する）"という表現は次のどの意味にいちばん近いですか？）
Pattern 2. The expression "put up with" in line xx probably means ...
（xx 行目、"put up with（〜我慢する）"という表現は ... という意味になる。）

▶ Multiple Passage （複数の文書）について
インスタントメッセージ、手紙、新聞記事、公文書、オフィスメモ、Eメール、広告、指示文などの2つか3つの複数の文書と5問の質問から成ります。
TOEIC® Test の最後にバーンと出題され、もうそこまで来るまでに疲労困憊した受験生を苦しめます。しかし、内容は他の reading material より難しくなく、特に Material 1 は簡単で短い資料が多いですから、ここであきらめず、頑張りましょう。必ず質問を先に読み、その答えになるキーワードを文中から拾うこと。
何回か受験した人は READING SECTION をこの最後の部分から始める人もいます。ただマークミスはくれぐれも気をつけて下さい。

Unit 2
Health

Key Expressions

Step 1　A 欄の語彙に合う訳を B 欄から選びましょう。

A.
1. brochure
2. provider
3. condition
4. specialize
5. phobia
6. reasonable
7. walk-in
8. coverage
9. examination
10. appointment

B.
a. 専門とする
b. 対象範囲；保障範囲
c. 検査；試験
d. パンフレット
e. 安い
f. 予約
g. 病状；症状
h. （インターネット接続する）業者
i. 恐怖症
j. 飛び入りで，予約なしで

Dialog: About Health Insurance

Step 2　Dialog の中の空白に Key Expressions から当てはまる言葉を選びましょう。必要ならば語形を変えて入れてください。

Sofia and Ali are talking about a new health insurance policy.

Ali: What am I going to do? I have to get all of these medical tests done, and I only have ten days to do it in. How am I ever going to schedule them all?

Sofia: Why are you in such a big hurry? What do you need them for?

Ali: My company is changing its insurance (A) (　　　　). We're moving to a new (B) (　　　　), and so everyone has to have a new baseline (C) (　　　　) and undergo all these tests.

Sofia: Maybe I can help. I know a clinic on Fern Street that (D) (　　　　) in testing and screening for different medical (E) (　　　　). You can usually get a/an (F) (　　　　) quickly, and they also take (G) (　　　　).

Ali: That sounds perfect. But they must be pretty expensive.

Sofia: No. They're fairly (H) (　　　　). But won't the insurance cover the fee?

Ali: I'm not really sure. Do you happen to have the clinic's information?

Sofia: I think I have a (I) (　　　　) in my desk. I'll look for it and bring it to you later.

Ali: Thanks. That'll be a big help. But I really hate going to the doctor. I have a (J) (　　　　) about needles.

Sofia: Oh, don't be such a baby.

Dialog Comprehension

Step 3　Dialog に関する次の質問に答えましょう。

1. Why is the man in such a hurry?
   (A) He is changing companies.
   (B) He does not have an appointment.
   (C) He needs several medical tests done quickly.

2. What is the advantage of using the clinic on Fern Street?
   (A) The clinic can get tests done quickly.
   (B) The clinic is in a convenient location.
   (C) It is a new provider.

LISTENING SECTION

PART 1 Photographs（写真描写問題）（2問）

文を聞いて写真と一番一致するものを (A) (B) (C) (D) から選びなさい。

1. (A) (B) (C) (D)

2. (A) (B) (C) (D)

PART 2 Question-Response（応答問題）（3問）

質問または文を聞いて、一番適当と思われる応答を (A) (B) (C) から選びなさい。

1. (A) (B) (C)   2. (A) (B) (C)   3. (A) (B) (C)

PART 3 Conversation（会話問題）（3問）

会話文を聞いて質問に対する一番適当と思われる答えを (A) (B) (C) (D) から選びなさい。

1 mile	2 miles	3 miles	4 miles	5 miles
White ribbon	Purple ribbon	Yellow ribbon	Blue ribbon	Red ribbon
$100	$300	$500	$750	$1000
No T-shirt	No T-shirt	Green T-shirt	Gold T-shirt	Red T-shirt

1. What are the man and the woman doing?
   (A) Running a marathon
   (B) Raising money for charity
   (C) Walking their dogs
   (D) Working for different charities

2. Look at the graphic. What does the woman have to do to get a ribbon and a T-shirt that are the same color?
   (A) She has to make $500 for the wildlife fund.
   (B) She has to walk only part of the way.
   (C) She has to sell $750 worth of goods.
   (D) She has to make it all the way to the end.

3. What does the man say he really wants to do?
   (A) Make a lot of money
   (B) Win the race
   (C) Get a T-shirt
   (D) Rescue a lost dog

Unit 2

PART 4 Talks （説明文問題）（3問）

次のアナウンスメントを聞いて、質問に対する一番適当と思われる答を (A) (B) (C) (D) から選びなさい。

1. What is being advertised?
   - (A) A cosmetic surgery clinic
   - (B) A pet hospital
   - (C) A credit card for health and beauty needs
   - (D) A new kind of health insurance for pets only

2. Which of the following statements is true about the advertised item?
   - (A) Users do not have to pay for six months.
   - (B) It is not approved by most doctors.
   - (C) It does not cover trips to the dentist.
   - (D) It can be used for people's as well as animals' health expenses.

3. What most likely is a "tummy tuck"?
   - (A) A kind of cosmetic surgery
   - (B) A dental treatment
   - (C) A type of medical care
   - (D) An eye doctor's examination

TOEICのための満点アプリ
PART 2 Question-Response

文頭の疑問詞をしっかり聞き取ろう。

PART 2 の 25 問中 7, 8 問は what, who, who (whose), which, when, where, why, how (how many, how+ 形容詞) などの WH Questions です。そして、これらの疑問詞は必ず文の初めにあり聞き落としやすいのです。聞き落とした人を引っ掛ける、疑問詞が選択肢としてあり、受験者を待ち構えていると言うわけです。

問題が読まれる間隔は約5秒です。この5秒という時間はテストの場では、有効に使えばかなり、次の設問に備える気分的余裕も持つことができます。余裕を持って文頭の疑問詞を聴き落とさないようにできるよう練習しましょう。

Q: Where did you go last night?　夕べはどこに行ってたの？
　(A) I went there at 9 p.m.　そこへ午後9時に行った。
　(B) I went there by bicycle.　そこへは自転車で行った。
　(C) I went to a concert.　コンサートに行った。
正解：(C)

この文では (A) の When, (B) の How, (C) Where に対する3つの選択肢があります。正解のためには疑問詞 Where を聞き逃してはなりません。

疑問詞を聞き逃さなければ、正解する確率はグーンと上がります。この形式に慣れれば、Listening Test の中では一番得点しやすいパートですから、ここで、文頭の疑問詞を聞き逃さないようにしましょう。

READING SECTION

Grammar Points
TOEIC 頻出のポイント：Tricky Prepositions　前置詞

▶ Point 1　前置詞は形容詞に付きます。

自分の意志を正しく伝えるためには、正しい前置詞を使いましょう。TOEIC PART 5, PART 6 の頻出ポイントです。

例：similar **to**, responsible **for**, kind **of**, pleased **with**, surprised **at**, shocked **by** など

時には一つの形容詞はいくつかの違った前置詞とくっつき、それによって意味が違ってきます。**good at drawing, good to her** などとフレーズで覚えましょう。

good + at/to/for/of -----
- a. Sally is good **at** drawing.
- b. Ms. Baxter is good **to** her staff.
- c. This software is good **for** analyzing sales trends.
- d. It was very good **of** you to consider our firm.

concerned with/about -----
- e. This seminar is concerned **with** quality control.
- f. Mr. Simmons is very concerned **about** the recent exchange-rate fluctuations.

angry + at, with/about -----
- g. Sam was angry **at/with** his co-workers today.
- h. Jerry was angry **about** not getting a bonus this year.

▶ Point 2　前置詞は動詞にも付きます。

look, bring, come, put などの動詞に前置詞が付いてイディオムになると、元の意味とは違った言葉になります。日常的なイディオムを覚えましょう。

i. Part of my job is to **look after** (= take care of) the welfare of new employees.

j. Joe **brought up** (= introduced) some very important points in the staff meeting.

k. Hal **came across** (= found unexpectedly) some mistakes while he was checking last month's accounts.

l. I **put off** (= postponed) my doctor's appointment until tomorrow.

m. The boss fired Bob because he could no longer **put up with** (= tolerate) Bob's persistent lateness.

Unit 2

Grammar Quiz (5問)

次の文を読んで、一番適当と思われる語を選びなさい。

1. Use these scissors to cut ------- the pattern for the dress you want to sew.
   (A) up
   (B) off
   (C) out
   (D) into

2. During the meeting, the boss got upset ------- his assistant looking at her cellphone.
   (A) to
   (B) on
   (C) toward
   (D) about

3. The baby is already growing ------- of the clothes we bought him last month!
   (A) up
   (B) out
   (C) into
   (D) in

4. Mr. Richards always takes great care ------- his tools to make sure they are in perfect condition.
   (A) of
   (B) about
   (C) to
   (D) for

5. The scientists are trying to figure out why bees are dying -------.
   (A) up
   (B) from
   (C) off
   (D) down

PART 5 Incomplete Sentences (短文穴埋め問題) (2問)

次の文の空欄に一番適当と思われる答を (A) (B) (C) (D) から選びなさい。

1. Because of all the burglaries in the neighborhood that have taken place recently, Mrs. Long has become very careful ------- leaving things in the car.
   (A) to
   (B) for
   (C) about
   (D) with

2. John went shopping and now has everything he thinks he ------- to get by if the big snowstorm really does hit our area.
   (A) buys
   (B) needs
   (C) used
   (D) relies

PART 6 Text Completion (長文穴埋め問題) (4問)

次の文の4つの空欄に一番適当と思われる答を (A) (B) (C) (D) から選びなさい。

Text: Product Information

There is a new and exciting vegetable turning up on plates in homes and restaurants everywhere. This formerly "boring" vegetable is suddenly flying ------- (1) the supermarket shelves and selling like hotcakes. What is it? Believe it or not, it's cauliflower. This versatile veggie can be mashed, roasted, or fried like a steak. Driven by consumers' interest in alternatives to white rice and white bread, demand for cauliflower has skyrocketed. It has been ------- (2) everything from starters to pizza crust. It makes an excellent substitute ------- (3) potatoes—and even for rice.

"Cauliflower rice" is made by running the cauliflower through a food processor and then lightly cooking the pieces in oil. It contains one-tenth the calories of white rice and is a good source of vitamin C. It's become so popular that some supermarkets are limiting customers to just two bags. ------- (4). So if you want to freshen up your dinner table, you can't go wrong with good old cauliflower.

1. (A) away
   (B) into
   (C) above
   (D) off

2. (A) turned into
   (B) turned up
   (C) turned on
   (D) turned around

3. (A) to
   (B) from
   (C) for
   (D) with

4. (A) Some customers are bringing their own bags so that they can take more cauliflower home.
   (B) Few customers buy real white rice these days, in fact.
   (C) Cauliflower now ranks fourth among the ten most popular vegetables.
   (D) Some supermarkets have decided to stop selling cauliflower altogether.

PART 7 Reading Comprehension （読解問題）（5問）

次の3つの文書を読んで、一番適当と思われる答を (A) (B) (C) (D) から選びなさい。

Material 1: Letter 1

Dear Doctor,

　I always enjoy reading your column in the newspaper, but I never thought that I would have a problem for you. I am writing to you today because I am concerned about my dog, a one-year-old mixed breed. Like most puppies, he has always had a tremendous appetite, but a while ago, he suddenly stopped eating. He used to love the puppy-mix food I was giving him, but now he just looks at it and turns away. It seems to me that he sometimes acts as if he feels sick or his stomach hurts. Also, when he goes outside, he tries to eat grass. Is he ill, or do I just need to change his diet? Is there some kind of supplement I should give him? I've tried giving him Happy Puppy vitamins, but they are chewable, and he refuses to chew them. I have never seen a puppy that does not want to chew things!

Sincerely,
Worried in Seattle

Material 2: Letter 2

Dear Worried,

You mentioned that your dog is one year old, so it is quite likely that he is ready to move from puppy-mix food to adult dog food. I am a little concerned, however because you say he is eating grass. That usually indicates stomach trouble. You should continue to try to give him the vitamins, perhaps by hiding it in a treat that he likes or in a chew toy. I recommend a supplement called Pup Up, which you can find in most pet stores. This supplement comes in liquid form, so you can use a dropper and give it to him by dropping it down his throat. I am also sending you my own special recipe for a dog food that you can make at home. It contains fish liver oil, which most dogs love. If your puppy continues eating grass, however, you should take him to an animal clinic for a thorough checkup.

Hoping this helps,
The Animal Doctor

Material 3: Letter 3

> Dear Doctor,
>
> Thank you for your advice. Unfortunately, my dog is still not very interested in eating. He likes the Pup Up vitamins and takes them without complaining, but he does not seem to want more solid food. I tried your recipe, and he will take a bite or two, but then he loses interest. He has stopped eating grass, though. Even so, I think I will take your suggestion and have him checked out at an animal hospital. Luckily, there is a good one in my neighborhood.

1. How does "Worried" know about the doctor?
    (A) "Worried" has visited the doctor's hospital.
    (B) They ran into each other at a pet store.
    (C) "Worried" has read the doctor's newspaper column.
    (D) They buy dog food at the same market.

2. What makes the doctor's dog food special?
    (A) "Worried"'s dog loves it.
    (B) It is designed especially for puppies.
    (C) You can hide it in a treat or toy.
    (D) Pet owners can make it themselves.

3. What does the doctor's recipe contain?
    (A) Fish oil
    (B) Puppy mix
    (C) Pup Up vitamins
    (D) Liquid vitamins

4. What is "Worried" still concerned about?
    (A) Her dog refuses to swallow the vitamins.
    (B) Her dog complains about the doctor's recipe.
    (C) He is still eating grass.
    (D) Her dog is still not eating normally.

5. What will "Worried" most likely do next?
    (A) Give her dog some solid food for adults.
    (B) Buy some chew toys for her dog.
    (C) Take her dog to a clinic.
    (D) Take the dog to the doctor's new paper.

Unit 3
Entertainment

Key Expressions

Step 1 A欄の語彙に合う訳をB欄から選びましょう。

A.
1. be postponed
2. impressed
3. produce (n)
4. mouth-watering
5. stall
6. vendors
7. have a weakness for
8. available
9. demonstrations
10. organic

B.
a. 感心する
b. 〜に弱い；好きで我慢できない
c. 実演
d. 売る人；商人
e. （商品が）売られている
f. 延期される
g. 有機生産物の
h. よだれの垂れそうな
i. 産物
j. 屋台

Dialog: Going to a Food Festival

Step 2 Dialogの中の空白にKey Expressionsから当てはまる言葉を選びましょう。必要ならば語形を変えて入れてください。

Betty and Steve are talking about an upcoming food festival.

Betty: Hey, Steve. Did you hear about the Hamptons Food Festival? It was supposed to be held last weekend, but it (A) (　　　　) to this weekend.

Steve: Right. Actually, I went last year and had a great time. I'm planning to go again this time.

Betty: Oh, really? What kind of things did they have there last year?

Steve: There were lots of farm (B) (　　　　) (C) (　　　　) selling stuff, as well as some (D) (　　　　) cooking (E) (　　　　).

Betty: How about that! I've been getting into (F) (　　　　) cooking recently, so that sounds like something I'd be really interested in.

Steve: I heard that at the festival two years ago there was a truffle oil (G) (　　　　). I hope it makes a comeback this year.

Betty: I (H) (　　　　) truffle oil myself. I'm never (I) (　　　　) with the brand they stock at my local supermarket, so I'd like to buy some at the festival—if it's (J) (　　　　).

Steve: Me, too. The thing is Betty, I have an extra ticket to the festival. Would you like to go together?

Betty: Sure, I'd love to! I could pick you up if you want. I just got a new car.
Steve: Really? I didn't know that. Sure, that sounds great.

Dialog Comprehension

Step 3　Dialog に関する次の質問に答えましょう。

1. What were festival attendees NOT able to do at last year's festival?
   (A) Purchase farm produce.
   (B) Watch cooking demonstrations.
   (C) Buy truffle oil.

2. What does Steve offer to do?
   (A) Give Betty a festival ticket.
   (B) Drive Betty to the festival.
   (C) Buy Betty some truffle oil.

LISTENING SECTION

PART 1　Photographs（写真描写問題）（2問）

文を聞いて写真と一番一致するものを (A) (B) (C) (D) から選びなさい。

1. (A) (B) (C) (D)　　　　　　　　2. (A) (B) (C) (D)

PART 2　Question-Response（応答問題）（3問）

質問または文を聞いて、一番適当と思われる応答を (A) (B) (C) から選びなさい。

1. (A) (B) (C)　　　2. (A) (B) (C)　　　3. (A) (B) (C)

Unit 3

PART 3 Conversation (会話問題) (3問)

会話文を聞いて質問に対する一番適当と思われる答えを (A) (B) (C) (D) から選びなさい。

1. What did the reviewers think of the *Zombie Killer* movies?
   (A) The reviews weren't too bad.
   (B) The reviews were all negative.
   (C) The films haven't been reviewed yet.
   (D) No one has heard what the reviewers have said about them.

2. What does Melody have to say about *Love and Marriage*?
   (A) She thinks it's much too long.
   (B) She doesn't care for the director.
   (C) She's been looking forward to seeing it.
   (D) It's no longer playing at any theater.

3. What will they most likely do?
   (A) Stay home and watch something on Netflix.
   (B) Go see Love and Marriage.
   (C) Go to the Lewis Mall Cineplex and check the schedule.
   (D) Go out for pizza.

PART 4 Talks (説明文問題) (3問)

次のアナウンスメントを聞いて、質問に対する一番適当と思われる答を (A) (B) (C) (D) から選びなさい。

Time	Show
12:45	Dolphin Magic
2:30	Sealion Spectacular
3:30	Penguin Parade
4:45	Shark Feeding Frenzy

1. How is the weather at the aquarium today?
   (A) It is sunny.
   (B) It is rainy.
   (C) It is hot and humid.
   (D) It is cloudy.

2. Look at the graphic. Which show will guests NOT be able to enjoy today?
   (A) The 12:45 show
   (B) The 2:30 show
   (C) The 3:30 show
   (D) The 4:45 show

3. What can customers with Dolphin Magic Show tickets do if they aren't able to attend other later shows?
   (A) They can get a refund.
   (B) They can exchange their tickets for earlier ones.
   (C) They can use their tickets on a different day.
   (D) They can file a claim with Customer Relations.

READING SECTION

Grammar Points
TOEIC 頻出ポイント：Essential Comparatives　大切な比較表現のいろいろ

この Book 2 では少し高度な比較級の文を学習しましょう。

▶ **Point 1 the more ..., the more の文型。**

比較級が 1 つの文に 2 つ入ります。

a. **The more** you sleep, **the better** you will feel.
b. **The longer** you look at a computer screen, **the more** tired your eyes become.
c. **The more** you play the game, **the better** you get at it.

▶ **Point 2 as ... as**

二つのことを as ... as を使って比べることができます。基本的にこの二つは同位だという意味になります。

d. ABC Corporation is **as good as** XYZ Corporation.
   ところが文に否定形 Not が入ってくると、話は全く違って、二つのものは対照的な意味を持つことになるのです。
e. ABC Corporation is **not as successful as** XYZ Corporation. = XYZ Corporation is **more successful than** ABC Corporation.
f. This year's growth rate is **not as good as** we expected. =This year's growth is worse than we expected.

▶ **Point 3 much more, far more, twice as much, slightly**

これらの表現を使うことで、二つの違いの大きさを表現することが出来ます。

g. ABC Corporation is **much/far/a lot more successful than** XYZ Corporation.
h. XYZ Corporation is **nowhere near as successful as** ABC Corporation.
i. ABC Corporation is **twice as successful as** XYZ Corporation.
j. Betty's salary is **slightly/a little/a bit less than** John's.

Grammar Quiz (5問)

次の文を読んで、一番適当と思われる語を選びなさい。

1. The more you sell, the ------- commission you will earn.
   (A) more
   (B) less
   (C) large
   (D) slight

2. Our sales record for this year is ------- near as bad as that of our rivals.
   (A) about
   (B) nowhere
   (C) just as
   (D) far more

3. The sequel to "Stop Time" earned ------- much at the box office as the original film.
   (A) twice as
   (B) double
   (C) less as
   (D) more than

4. The more people who watch our program, the ------- the show's rating becomes.
   (A) fewer
   (B) more
   (C) higher
   (D) larger

5. This new alternative reality game is ------- more fun than regular ones.
   (A) less than
   (B) a lot
   (C) not as
   (D) nowhere near

Unit 3

33

PART 5 Incomplete Sentences (短文穴埋め問題) (2問)

次の文の空欄に一番適当と思われる答を (A) (B) (C) (D) から選びなさい。

1. At this year's video-game conference, Masakazu Hasegawa is expected to unveil "Super Sunshine," his much ------- game that has been in development for over five years.
   - (A) anticipate
   - (B) anticipates
   - (C) anticipated
   - (D) anticipating

2. Is locking up the office at night ------- his responsibility as hers?
   - (A) as many
   - (B) as much
   - (C) as important
   - (D) as necessary

PART 6 Text Completion (長文穴埋め問題) (4問)

次の文の4つの空欄に一番適当と思われる答を (A) (B) (C) (D) から選びなさい。

Text: Notice

Attention all patrons of the Maxwell Kent Theater Company:
We will be undertaking extensive renovations throughout the summer. We will be ------- (1.) the dressing rooms, adding a new bar lounge area in the atrium, and increasing our seating capacity from 1,500 to 2,000 seats, which will involve a ------- (2.) redesign of the main theater. We expect the dressing rooms to be completed by the middle of July, and the bar lounge to be open for business by the beginning of August. We are not sure how long the seating increase will take, but work is ------- (3.) to be finished by late September. This is subject to change, however. ------- (4.)

1. (A) rehabilitating
   (B) reviewing
   (C) remodeling
   (D) reviving

2. (A) partial
   (B) partly
   (C) parted
   (D) part

3. (A) resolved
   (B) concluded
   (C) decided
   (D) estimated

4. (A) We anticipate huge crowds to enjoy our plays during this period.
   (B) If you would like to audition for any of our summer productions, go to our website.
   (C) We appreciate your cooperation and patience during this time.
   (D) We are pleased to announce our upcoming summer-season line-up of great plays.

Unit 3

PART 7 Reading Comprehension （読解問題）（5 問）

次の3つの文書を読んで、一番適当と思われる答を (A) (B) (C) (D) から選びなさい。

Material 1: Text message

Conversation between two people about joining a book club at a local community center

Stephanie: Hey, Jennifer. You enjoy reading, right? Sabrina and I were thinking about joining a book club. How about you?

Jennifer: Great idea. Coincidentally, just the other day I saw an online announcement for book clubs at a local community center. I'll send it to you now.

Jennifer: So what do you think?

Stephanie: They both look interesting! Sabrina and I read pretty much anything, so I think either one would suit us. What about you?

Jennifer: I'm mostly a fantasy and sci-fi fan, so I would prefer the Sci-Fi Fantasy Circle. But I'm open to other genres, too.

Stephanie: The Sci-Fi Fantasy Circle sounds fine to me. And I'm sure Sabrina be OK with it. Shall I sign us up for that?

Jennifer: Oh ... wait. It says here that they meet on Saturday afternoons. I sometimes have to work on Saturday, so I don't think I could make it to all of the meetings.

Stephanie: What about Bookworms Anonymous, then? It seems to have more of a variety. They say they read all genres.

Jennifer: But those are contemporary novels, and, to be honest, I prefer classic sci-fi. Oh well. I guess it won't hurt if I miss a meeting now and then.

Material 2: Online announcement for book clubs

Sci-Fi Fantasy Circle
Time: Saturdays, 1p.m.-3p.m
Place: First-floor Recreation Room

Are you interested in Science Fiction and Fantasy? Come on down to the Sci-Fi Fantasy Circle! We read and discuss a range of classics, including J.R.R. Tolkien, Frederick Pohl, and Isaac Asimov. New members welcome. *

Bookworms Anonymous
Time: Sundays, 3p.m.-5p.m.
Place: Second-floor Library

Want to discuss the latest bestsellers? Come and join us at Bookworms Anonymous! Every month, we read the newest releases, covering all fiction genres. From King to Murakami to Anne Tyler: there is always something guaranteed to satisfy your booklover's appetite! New members welcome.**

For details on how to sign up, please email librarian@lumpsfieldcommunitycenter.org

* Limited spaces left
**Only two more spaces left

Material 3:

E-mail
To: librarian@lumpsfieldcommunitycenter.org
From: Stephanie (ssofy@almondmail.com)
Subject: Book clubs

To whom it may concern,
My name is Stephanie Sofy, and some friends and I are interested in joining one of the community center's book clubs. Before we join though, I have a few questions.

According to your website, the Sci-Fi Fantasy Circle meets on Saturdays, but is that every weekend? One of my friends sometimes works on Saturdays, and will not be able to make it from time to time. If it is every Saturday, is it okay to skip meetings from time to time?

Also, do we have to buy all the books we read? I know the meetings take place in the community center, so I'm wondering if we can borrow books from the center's library. But there seem to be quite a few members, so I guess that there might not be enough copies for any given book. It might be a little expensive for us to buy new books every month, so is there any other option? Thank you for reading this, and have a good day.

Regards,
Stephanie Sofy

1. What kind of books does Stephanie enjoy?
   (A) Science fiction
   (B) Fantasy
   (C) Only the newest releases
   (D) Any genre

2. What kind of books does Bookworms Anonymous focus on?
   (A) Contemporary works
   (B) Classic science fiction
   (C) Women's fiction
   (D) Novels by King, Murakami, and Tyler

Unit 3

3. What is Stephanie's concern about joining a book club?
   (A) The cost of the books to be read
   (B) How much time it will take to read each book
   (C) The number of spaces left
   (D) The location of the community center

4. What is the meaning of the underlined phrase "from time to time" in Stephanie's email 2nd paragraph, 3rd line?
   (A) Consistently
   (B) Rarely
   (C) Occasionally
   (D) Frequently

5. Which book club will Stephanie and her friends most likely join?
   (A) The Sci-Fi Fantasy Circle
   (B) Bookworms Anonymous
   (C) Neither the Sci-Fi Fantasy Circle nor Bookworms Anonymous
   (D) Both the Sci-Fi Fantasy Circle and Bookworms Anonymous

---

TOEIC のための満点アプリ
PART 7 Reading Comprehension 読解問題

実際のテストでは 54 問を約 50 分で解答しなければなりません。ということはすべての文章を丁寧に読んでいる時間はありませんから、次のようなステップで要領よく解答する技を身につけましょう。

▶ **scanning で時間を短縮しよう**

Step 1- パッセージのタイトル、レターヘッド、差出人、用件などを見る。
どういう種類の内容かが推察できます。

Step 2- それからすぐに質問のキーワードを scan する。

Step 3- 質問のキーワードと選択肢をにらみながら、本文を scan して、該当する答を見つけ出す。
この時、1) 手で問題文のページを覆ったりしないこと、2) 全ページを視野に入れること。
ページ全体に目を配りながら、本文中にある答を見つけるようにしましょう。

Unit 4
Going House Hunting

Key Expressions

Step 1　A欄の語彙に合う訳をB欄から選びましょう。

A.
1. deal
2. cramped
3. spacious
4. affordable
5. rent
6. (be) occupied
7. sign a lease
8. real estate agent
9. security deposit
10. studio apartment

B.
a. 狭苦しい
b. ワンルームマンション
c. 保証金
d. 不動産業者
e. 契約を結ぶ
f. 取引き
g. 広々とした
h. 値段が手頃な
i. 住んでいる
j. 家賃

Dialog: Comfort or Convenience

Step 2　Dialogの中の空白にKey Expressionsから当てはまる言葉を選びましょう。必要ならば語形を変えて入れてください。

Rachel and Yoji are discussing pros and cons of the apartments.

Rachel: Wow! Yoji, your apartment is … what's the word? (A) (　　　　)!

Yoji: Don't rub it in! But a (B) (　　　　) is all I can afford in this area. It's pretty high-end.

Rachel: The area where I live has some nice (C) (　　　　) duplexes, and they all have at least two bedrooms.

Yoji: That definitely sounds intriguing. How far from the city center are they?

Rachel: Well, they are a little far out, but I think it's worth it to live in a more (D) (　　　　) place.

Yoji: Hmm. How much are they per month? And what about the (E) (　　　　)?

Rachel: I was able to get a great deal from my (F) (　　　　), so I only pay $800 (G) (　　　　) with no extra charges for utilities. And only $200 for a deposit, which I get back when I move out.

Yoji: Wow! That's a great (H) (　　　　). Could you introduce me to your agent?

38

Rachel: I'd be happy to! Now that I think about it, the unit across from mine isn't (I) (　　　　) at the moment.

Yoji: If I could hurry up and (J) (　　　　), we would be neighbors!

Rachel: Wouldn't that be nice? I'll give them a call!

Dialog Comprehension

Step 3　Dialog に関する次の質問に答えましょう。

1. Why does Yoji live in such a small apartment?
    (A) The area is expensive.
    (B) He doesn't need much space since he lives alone.
    (C) No other rooms were available.

2. What will Rachel do now?
    (A) She will think Yoji's request over.
    (B) She will ask about the rent and security deposit.
    (C) She will contact her real estate agent.

LISTENING SECTION

PART 1 Photographs （写真描写問題）（2問）

文を聞いて写真と一番一致するものを (A) (B) (C) (D) から選びなさい。

1. (A) (B) (C) (D)

2. (A) (B) (C) (D)

PART 2 Question-Response （応答問題）（3問）

質問または文を聞いて、一番適当と思われる応答を (A) (B) (C) から選びなさい。

1. (A) (B) (C)   2. (A) (B) (C)   3. (A) (B) (C)

PART 3 Conversation （会話問題）（3問）

会話文を聞いて質問に対する一番適当と思われる答えを (A) (B) (C) (D) から選びなさい。

	Item	Price	Maker	Fabric
A set	2-piece lounge suite	$699.99	Radford's	*Additional charges for fabrics.
B set	2-piece sectional sofa	$1,699.99	Dagostino	Polyester: $20 per set
C set	3-piece lounge suite	$1,799.99	Dagostino	Synthetic suede: $70 per set
D set	3-piece lounge suite	$999.99	Radford's	Genuine leather: $100 per set

1. Look at the graphic. How much will the shopper pay for his new set?
   (A) $699.99
   (B) $719.99
   (C) $769.99
   (D) $1,799.99

2. When will the shopper receive the set he wants to have order made?
   (A) The salesperson isn't sure.
   (B) A week from today.
   (C) It will be ready when he moves in to his new place.
   (D) It will take at least three weeks.

3. Why most likely has the shopper selected the set he has ordered?
   (A) It is more suitable for children.
   (B) He doesn't really care for leather.
   (C) He thinks his wife will like it better.
   (D) The salesperson talks him into it.

Unit 4

PART 4 Talks （説明文問題）（3問）

次のアナウンスメントを聞いて、質問に対する一番適当と思われる答を (A) (B) (C) (D) から選びなさい。

1. Why is Ray calling Mary?
   (A) To report a problem with the kitchen set
   (B) To offer her a discount on her purchase
   (C) To inform her that her order is ready for delivery
   (D) To inform her of a shipping delay

2. At which of these times can Mary NOT get her kitchen set delivered?
   (A) Monday at 5:00 P.M.
   (B) Wednesday at 9:00 A.M.
   (C) Friday at 6:00 P.M
   (D) Saturday at 10:00 A.M.

3. By when does Mary need to decide the installation option?
   (A) By 5:00 P.M. the day after tomorrow
   (B) Two days before her selected delivery date and time
   (C) By 9:00 A.M. on Sunday
   (D) Within one week of Ray's call

TOEIC のための満点アプリ
PART 4 Talks 説明文問題

問題数 30 問。いろいろなトピックに関する 10 のアナウンスメントがあり、それぞれ 3 つの設問があります。どちらかというと日本では PART 3 の会話形式より PART 4 のような文章形式の英語に触れる機会の方が多いですから、日頃から英文書類を書いたり読んだりしている人にとっては、PART 3 よりかえって得点しやすいかもしれません。しかしやはり、LISTENING SECTION 中では、難しい語彙が一番多く、読まれる速度もナチュラルスピードですから、かなり頻繁に英文を耳から聞いてないと高得点が難しいところです。ですから TOEIC700 点以上を目指す人はテスト前によく shadowing をして、60％以上得点をめざしましょう。

▶まずは質問を読もう
Step 1- アナウンスメントが始まる前に必ず質問を読む習慣を身につけましょう。
Step 2- 質問は、アナウンスメントの順序に沿って出題されているので、質問のキーワードをにらみながら、アナウンスメントを聞いていきましょう。
これだと思ったら迷わず、即、マークシートをチェックしましょう。

▶アナウンスメントの内容はビジネスに関するものや公共関係です

▶質問の種類は、大きい質問、小さい質問、数字に関する質問などがあります

▶大きい質問はアナウンスメントの要約に関するものです

READING SECTION

Grammar Points
TOEIC 頻出ポイント：Articles and Quantifiers　冠詞と数量詞

▶ Point 1　不特定なものを指す不定冠詞とその複数形

不特定なものを指す単数形は **a/an** をつける -----　　*a.* I want to buy **an** apartment.
不特定なものを指す複数形は冠詞がない -----　　　　*b.* I prefer **cats** to **dogs**.

▶ Point 2　特定なものを指す定冠詞

特定なものを指す単数形 -----　　*c.* My parents live in **the** apartment next door to mine.
特定なものを指す複数形 -----　　*d.* **The** cats in my neighborhood are very noisy.

▶ Point 3　数量詞：可算名詞と不可算名詞

数量詞とは、ものの数や量を表すときに使う形容詞または副詞で、**all, each, every, some, any, both, most, least, more, less, few, little, no, none** などがあります。可算名詞または、不可算名詞としか使えないものがあります。

<u>可算名詞</u>	<u>不可算名詞</u>
many	much
(a) few	(a) little/a bit
a (great) number of	a great amount of
fewer/fewest	less/least
several	a great deal of

▶ Point 4　間違いやすい数量詞

1. **little** (=not much) と **a little**, **few** (=not many) と **a few** の違いに気をつけよう。

    e. There is **little** hope that the economy will improve by the end of the year.

    f. **Few** people are capable of becoming Olympic athletes.

2. both「両方とも」、either は「どちらか」neither は「どちらでもない」

    g. I like **both** A **and** B.

    h. You can take **either** A **or** B.

    i. I like **neither** A **nor** B.

Grammar Quiz (5問)

次の文を読んで、一番適当と思われる語を選びなさい。

1. I prefer ------- to houses.
   - (A) apartments
   - (B) an apartment
   - (C) apartment
   - (D) the apartment

2. ------- people who live in this town are very friendly.
   - (A) A
   - (B) The
   - (C) Every
   - (D) Much

3. The apartments on the fourth floor have the ------- rooms.
   - (A) many
   - (B) few
   - (C) most
   - (D) some

4. ------- of the apartments that I looked at today was right for me.
   - (A) No
   - (B) Less
   - (C) Little
   - (D) None

5. ------- of the houses has an air conditioner.
   - (A) All
   - (B) Little
   - (C) Some
   - (D) Neither

PART 5 Incomplete Sentences (短文穴埋め問題)（2問）

次の文の空欄に一番適当と思われる答を (A) (B) (C) (D) から選びなさい。

1. The blueprints for our client's new house have been -------.
    (A) deliver
    (B) delivered
    (C) delivery
    (D) delivers

2. Bamsford Realty specializes in ------- housing for high-income earners.
    (A) ordinary
    (B) bargain
    (C) luxurious
    (D) sufficient

PART 6 Text Completion (長文穴埋め問題)（4問）

次の文の4つの空欄に一番適当と思われる答を (A) (B) (C) (D) から選びなさい。

Text: Article

Nowadays, millennials are having a harder time ---1--- the property market. There are several reasons for this. The first is that the average wage has not ---2--- at the same rate that property prices have. Another reason is that more millennials are choosing to rent than own. This has created a generation marked by instability and ---3---. Because paying rent affects their ability to save for a home of their own, some millennials are choosing to remain in their parents' houses. ---4---

1. (A) deciding
   (B) choosing
   (C) entering
   (D) revealing

2. (A) rise
   (B) risen
   (C) rose
   (D) rising

3. (A) uncertainty
   (B) unconsciousness
   (C) unwillingness
   (D) unreasonableness

4. (A) Their parents' homes are already overcrowded, in fact.
   (B) Thus, they can never achieve true happiness.
   (C) Eventually, however the property market is expected to recover.
   (D) As a result, they are also putting off getting married and having children.

Unit 4

PART 7 Reading Comprehension （読解問題）（5 問）

次の 2 つの文書を読んで、一番適当と思われる答を (A) (B) (C) (D) から選びなさい。

Material 1: Letter 1

Dear Mr. Styles:

A client of mine who recently returned to England after a two-year stay in New York City highly recommended you and your company to me. I will soon be sending two of my staff to New York for an 18-month period to set up a branch office there. As the employees will both be accompanied by their families, it is imperative that we find each of them an apartment suitable for a family of five. We would also prefer that the apartments be furnished. My company is prepared to pay up to $3,000 per month for each unit. Proximity to our company's new office and to public transposition must be taken into consideration, as well. I am also wondering if there is a possibility of receiving a discount because we will be renting two units. I would appreciate it if you would get back to me on this matter as soon as possible.

Sincerely yours,
Helen Deville
Human resources Director
Manning Financial Services

Material 2: Letter 2

Dear Ms. Deville,

Thank you for your letter. I am confident that we will be able to assist you with this matter. I have attached some information below. Please look it over and let me know what you think. I am looking forward to hearing from you.

Regards,
Henry Styles
Apartment coordinator
RAD Living

Newly-renovated apartment units in Astoria, Queens.
  * 3-bedrooms, $2,500/month (plus 1 month-rent as deposit)
  * Ideal location, just seven minutes away from Steinway Street station.
  * State-of-the-art security system, CCTV, and security on premises
  * Apartments include air conditioning, kitchen appliances, and furniture
  * On-street parking available (a private parking space is also available for an additional fee)
  * Close to shops and restaurants
  * 24-month lease - negotiable

1. Who needs apartments for living in New York?
   (A) Henry Styles
   (B) Helen Deville's client
   (C) Manning's Financial employees
   (D) Helen Deville herself

2. What seems to be most important for Helen Deville?
   (A) Space
   (B) Cost
   (C) Location
   (D) Decor

3. Which point will Helen Deville most likely bring up for negotiation with Henry Styles?
   (A) Decreasing the rent.
   (B) Renovating the rooms.
   (C) Increasing the number of apartments.
   (D) Shortening the length of the lease.

4. What information is NOT included in the apartment listing?
   (A) Proximity to shopping and transportation
   (B) Distance from the new office
   (C) The apartments' amenities
   (D) Security facilities

5. How much will Helen Deville's company need to pay for the two apartments for the first month?
   (A) $2,500
   (B) $5,000
   (C) $7,500
   (D) $10,000

Unit 5
Ecology

Key Expressions

Step 1　A 欄の語彙に合う訳を B 欄から選びましょう。

A.
1. eco-warrior
2. in the long run
3. carbon emissions
4. benefits
5. hazardous
6. rebates
7. pollution-free
8. electricity bill
9. installation cost
10. promising

B.
a. 報奨金；払い戻し
b. 電気料金
c. 環境保護活動家；環境戦士
d. 汚染のない
e. 長期的に見れば
f. 取り付け費用；建築費
g. 長所；良い点
h. 見込みがある；有望な
i. 害のある；危険な
j. 炭酸ガス排出

Dialog: Switching Energy Sources

Step 2　Dialog の中の空白に Key Expressions から当てはまる言葉を選びましょう。必要ならば語形を変えて入れてください。

Jack has just stopped by Margaret's place. Margaret has brochures spread out all over her living room floor.

Jack: Hey, Margaret, what are all these brochures for?

Margaret: I'm thinking of switching to solar energy. The local power plant relies on coal, which, as you know, is (A) (　　　　) to the environment.

Jack: Wow, you're a true (B) (　　　　)! But are there really any (C) (　　　　) to solar energy?

Margaret: Lots of them. According to these brochures, solar energy produces the least amount of (D) (　　　　) of all energy sources. And because Florida has a semi-tropical climate, we don't have to worry about a lack of sunlight.

Jack: Which means that your (E) (　　　　) will be cheaper, too! Hmm, maybe I should give solar energy a try.

Margaret: We can go have a consultation together! Solar energy is cheaper (F) (　　　　), but I am a little concerned about the (G) (　　　　) of the solar panels. They can run as high as $20,000!

Jack: But look. This pamphlet says that many local governments offer (H) (　　　　) for installing solar panels.

Margaret: I saw that, too. That sounds really (I) (　　　　)! Let's look into that, as well.

Jack: Excellent plan! It says here that there's a solar-energy consultant office just ten minutes from here. If you'd like, I can drive you there.

Margaret: Or better yet, we can ride our bicycles. Cycling is (J) (　　　　)!

Dialog Comprehension

Step 3　Dialog に関する次の質問に答えましょう。

1. What is the main reason Margaret is considering switching to solar energy?
   (A) It is cheaper than energy produced from coal.
   (B) She lives in an area with a lot of sunlight.
   (C) It is a less environmentally harmful alternative to other energy sources.

2. How will Jack and Margaret most likely go to the solar-energy consultation office?
   (A) By car
   (B) By bicycle
   (C) On foot

LISTENING SECTION

PART 1 Photographs（写真描写問題）（2問）

文を聞いて写真と一番一致するものを (A) (B) (C) (D) から選びなさい。

1. (A) (B) (C) (D)　　　　2. (A) (B) (C) (D)

Unit 5

PART 2 Question-Response（応答問題）（3問）

質問または文を聞いて、一番適当と思われる応答を (A) (B) (C) から選びなさい。

1. (A) (B) (C)   2. (A) (B) (C)   3. (A) (B) (C)

PART 3 Conversation（会話問題）（3問）

会話文を聞いて質問に対する一番適当と思われる答えを (A) (B) (C) (D) から選びなさい。

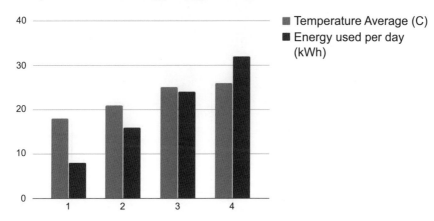

Temperature and energy usage in Belleville

1. Where do the speakers most likely work?
    (A) A public power utility
    (B) A meteorological agency
    (C) A polling company
    (D) A university research lab

2. Which factor do the speakers want primarily to deal with?
    (A) Temperature rises
    (B) Energy usage by consumers
    (C) Both temperature rises and energy usage
    (D) Neither temperature rises nor energy usage

3. Look at the graph. Which number represents August?
    (A) 1
    (B) 2
    (C) 3
    (D) 4

49

PART 4 Talks （説明文問題）（3問）

次のアナウンスメントを聞いて、質問に対する一番適当と思われる答を (A) (B) (C) (D) から選びなさい。

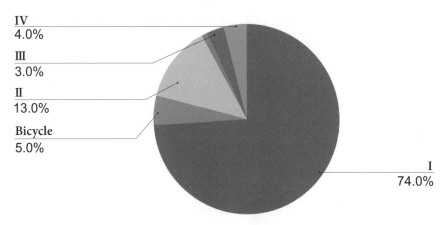

How do you travel to work?

1. How do most survey respondents get to work?
   (A) By car
   (B) By bus
   (C) By train
   (D) By bicycle

2. Look at the graph. Which numeral represents the people who take the bus to work?
   (A) I
   (B) II
   (C) III
   (D) IV

3. What does the speaker think viewers should do?
   (A) Trade in their automobiles.
   (B) Respond to the survey question.
   (C) Tune into the news program.
   (D) Use alternative means of transportation besides driving to work.

READING SECTION

Grammar Points

TOEIC 頻出のポイント：**Participles**　分詞構文 ~ing と ~ed

英語には現在分詞 ~ing と、過去分詞 ~ed と 2 種類の分詞形があります。

▶ **Point 1**　名詞の前に置いて形容詞として使います。

a. I'll never forget my brother's **scared** face when he saw a big snake.
b. I love the smell of **chopped** onion.

▶ **Point 2**　~ing と ~ed では意味が違う。

TOEIC PART 5, 6 頻出ポイントです。interesting book と interested customer

c. I read an **interesting book** over the summer holiday.
d. After explaining the product's details, one **interested customer** asked me about the price.

▶ **Point 3**　分詞として主語を形容します。

e. **Astonished**, Bob looked at the news report of the hurricane's destruction.
f. **Crying**, Daniela mourned the loss of her grandmother.

▶ **Point 4**　分詞構文形は長くなることもあります。

g. **Cycling** around town, Todd ran into his friend Percy.
h. **Shocked** by the news of her favorite TV show's cancellation, Betsy wrote an angry e-mail to the station.

▶ **Point 5**　受動態の分詞構文もあります。

i. **Having been chosen** to represent their city, the students did their best in the debate contest.

▶ **Point 6**　主語が一致しない時には分詞形は使えません。

j. × Waiting for the train for half an hour, it finally showed up.
　○ **I** waited for the train for over half an hour, and **it** finally showed up.

▶ **Point 7**　分詞形は名詞の後に付いて、関係詞としての役目もします。

k. Vegetables (that have been) **steamed** in a steamer are more nutritious.
l. The woman (who is) **giving** the talk is the new CEO.

Grammar Quiz (5問)

次の文を読んで、一番適当と思われる語を選びなさい。

1. I refuse to read another ------- book for this class!
   (A) bore
   (B) boring
   (C) bored
   (D) boredom

2. -------, Billy ran to the stage to receive his award.
   (A) Amazed
   (B) Amazing
   (C) Amaze
   (D) Amazement

3. ------- through the second-hand bookstore, I came across a rare first edition of *Bleak House*.
   (A) Browse
   (B) Browses
   (C) Browsing
   (D) Browsed

4. Having been ------- for the $15,000 scholarship, I couldn't help shouting for joy.
   (A) choose
   (B) choice
   (C) chose
   (D) chosen

5. Students who ------- in class are not only disruptive, but also just plain rude!
   (A) talking
   (B) talk
   (C) talks
   (D) talked

Unit 5

PART 5 Incomplete Sentences（短文穴埋め問題）（2問）

次の文の空欄に一番適当と思われる答を (A) (B) (C) (D) から選びなさい。

1. We need to ------- energy in order to reduce our carbon footprint.
   - (A) consume
   - (B) conserve
   - (C) conduct
   - (D) concentrate

2. The world's polar ice caps and glaciers will melt away if the atmosphere keeps -------.
   - (A) heating up
   - (B) going up
   - (C) hotting up
   - (D) warm up

PART 6 Text Completion（長文穴埋め問題）（4問）

次の文の4つの空欄に一番適当と思われる答を (A) (B) (C) (D) から選びなさい。

Text: Article

When you think of pollution, what comes to mind? Most people will think of air or water pollution. But did you know that light—the artificial light of modern life—can be a ------- (1.) of pollution as well? Light can disrupt the earth's ecological balance in several ways. Many nocturnal animals, for example, get confused by artificial lights, which alters their sleep patterns for the ------- (2.). Artificial light can also affect human sleep patterns. When we sleep, our bodies produce a chemical called melatonin, which is best produced when our surroundings are ------- (3.). If there is too much light around us, our bodies can't and won't produce sufficient melatonin, and, as a consequence, we can't and won't sleep nearly as well. ------- (4.)

1. (A) source
   (B) provider
   (C) supplier
   (D) birthplace

2. (A) better
   (B) worse
   (C) bad
   (D) worst

3. (A) bright
   (B) quiet
   (C) dark
   (D) noisy

4. (A) My point is that something needs to be done to reduce light pollution for both animals' and humans' sake.
   (B) I really feel sorry for those animals that don't get enough sleep during the day.
   (C) Noise pollution, which occurs when there is too much noise, is not nearly so serious an environmental problem as air pollution.
   (D) Together, air, water, and light pollution are making my life miserable.

PART 7 Reading Comprehension （読解問題）（5問）

次の3つの文書を読んで、一番適当と思われる答を (A) (B) (C) (D) から選びなさい。

Material 1: Advertisement

If an ecotour sounds exciting to you, why not sail to the islands that started it all? Come see all the exotic plants and animal species of the Galapagos Islands, and trod the path the great naturalist Charles Darwin walked nearly two centuries ago.

What the Galapagos Islands particularly offer is sustainable tourism. What is that, you may ask? Sustainable tourism is travel that strives to preserve local habitats. For all our tours, we do everything possible to conserve water and energy, recycle and treat waste material, hire local employees—and pay them a fair wage. Join one of our tours, and you too can experience the Galapagos Islands in a sustainable, eco-friendly way.

Our islands were designated a UNESCO World Heritage Site in 1979. We are proud of these beautiful, timeless islands and will do whatever we can to help you plan your trip. We will show you when and how to get here, what to bring with you, and where to stay. So don't hesitate: Plan your Galapagos sustainable adventure today!

Material 2: Accommodation information

Beachside Eco-villas
Packages include:
- room with guaranteed ocean view
- three meals a day (alcoholic drinks not included)
- free shuttle bus between hotel and airport

Rates:
Dry season (June 1 - November 30) - From $440
Wet season (December 1 - May 31) - From $320

   * Rates are per person per night.
  ** Add an extra $50 fee per person for stays during peak seasons (June 15 - September 10 and December 15 - January 15)
 *** Guests who choose to opt out of our housekeeping services will receive a 10 percent discount on their total accommodation costs.

Unit 5

Material 3:

E-mail
From: Chloe Minogue
To: Maxine Spears
Subject: Galapagos Islands Ecotour
Date: February 26
Hi Maxine, I've been thinking about college graduation trip that we discussed the other day, and I've come up with a great idea. Since we're both evolutionary biology majors, why don't we celebrate our four years of hard work by treating ourselves to an ecotour of the Galapagos Islands? I've wanted to go there ever since I visited Ecuador with my sister in high school and our host family recommended it. I've found some excellent deals online, so even with our humble budgets, we should be able to stay for at least a night or two. After that we can crash at my old host family's house in Ecuador, which is lovely, by the way. With proper planning, we could be in the islands within two or three weeks after graduation, on May 20. It would be best if we could avoid the peak season price hike. Let me know what you think. Chloe

1. What is NOT mentioned in the advertisement as a feature of sustainable tourism?
   (A) Preservation of water and energy
   (B) Responsible garbage disposal
   (C) Fair employment practices
   (D) Working side by side with local people

2. When are Chloe and Maxine most likely to visit the Galapagos Islands?
   (A) The beginning of May
   (B) The end of May
   (C) The beginning of June
   (D) The end of June

3. How did Chloe first find out about the Galapagos Islands?
   (A) From an internet website
   (B) From her sister, who lives in Ecuador
   (C) From her host family in Ecuador
   (D) From her biology professor

4. What does Chloe mean when she says "we can crash at my host family's house"?
   (A) They can stay there for a while.
   (B) They can pay them a nice, long visit.
   (C) They can borrow some money from them, if necessary.
   (D) They can drop in on them unexpectedly.

5. How might Maxine and Chloe save some money during their time in the Galapagos Islands?
   (A) By staying with a local family
   (B) By bringing and cooking their own food
   (C) By not using private transportation
   (D) By not using hotel housekeeping services

TOEICのための満点アプリ
PART 3 Conversations 会話問題

会話に関する大きい質問（大意に関する質問）と小さい質問（細かい情報に関する質問）があります。必ず会話の始まる前の少しの間に、質問に目を通しておきましょう。

Man: Would it be possible to get on an earlier flight?
Woman: There's a 3 o'clock flight leaving in half an hour. Let me check for seat availability. Yes! There's one seat available. You can make it if you check in now.
Man: OK. I'll take it. And I only have a backpack for my carry-on.
Woman: Very good. Here's your boarding pass, sir.

大きい質問　1. Who are the two speakers?
   (A) A cabin attendant and a passenger
   (B) A customs officer and a traveler
   (C) An airline agent and a customer*

大きい質問　2. What does the man want?
   (A) To leave earlier than scheduled*
   (B) To cancel his flight
   (C) To pay cash for his ticket

小さい質問　What time is it now most likely?
   (A) 2:30 p.m.*
   (B) 2:45 p.m.
   (C) 3:30 p.m.

Review Test 1 (Units 1-5)

LISTENING SECTION (20 questions)

PART 1 Photographs （写真描写問題）（2問）

文を聞いて次の写真と一番一致する文を選びなさい。

1. (A) (B) (C) (D)   2. (A) (B) (C) (D)

PART 2　Question-Response （応答問題）（6問）

質問または文を聞いて、一番適当と思われる応答を (A) (B) (C) から選びなさい。

3. (A) (B) (C)   4. (A) (B) (C)   5. (A) (B) (C)
6. (A) (B) (C)   7. (A) (B) (C)   8. (A) (B) (C)

PART 3　Conversations （会話問題）（2 Converssation × 3 問＝ 6 問）

会話文を聞いて質問に対する一番適当と思われる答を (A) (B) (C) (D) から選びなさい。

Conversation 1:

9. What was the man's job at Maxie?
    (A) He was a software engineer.
    (B) He was on the board of derectors.
    (C) He was a manual laborer
    (D) He was a technical writer.

10. Why did he leave Maxie?
    (A) Maxie hired an outside company to do his job.
    (B) Maxie went out of business.
    (C) He preferred to work for WonderTech.
    (D) He was asked to take a salary cut.

11. What was the result of his job interview at WonderTech?
    (A) They asked him to provide more references.
    (B) He was offered a job as a technical writer.
    (C) They want him to come in for a second interview.
    (D) They will look at his writing and let him know their decision.

表を見ながら会話文を聞いて質問に対する一番適当と思われる答を (A) (B) (C) (D) から選びなさい。

Conversation 2:

System	Price	Storage	Resolution
NS	$299.99	32 Gigabytes	1080p
S4	$299.99	30 Gigabytes*	1080p
S4 Premium	$399.99	100 Gigabytes	2160p

*Hard Drive space is upgradeable (additional hard drive sold separately)

12. What is the shopper most concerned about?
    (A) Price
    (B) Storage space
    (C) Resolution
    (D) Popularity

13. What additional device would be required for the man's daughter to use the S4 Premium system?
    (A) A separate hard drive
    (B) A less powerful TV set
    (C) A more recent-model TV
    (D) A larger screen

14. Look at the chart. Which system is the shopper most likely to buy?
    (A) The NS
    (B) The S4
    (C) The S4 Premium
    (D) He will not buy any of them.

Review Test 1 (Units 1-5)

PART 4　Talks （説明文問題）（3問）（2 Talks × 3問＝6問）

次のアナウンスメントを聞いて、質問に対する一番適当と思われる答を (A) (B) (C) (D) から選びなさい。

Announcement 1:

15. Who will attend this event?
    (A) Company employees only
    (B) Company employees and their families
    (C) It is open to the general public.
    (D) Midnight concert-goers

16. What prize will the winner of the pie-eating contest receive?
    (A) Tickets to a concert
    (B) Tickets to the midnight fireworks show
    (C) Tickets to a baseball game
    (D) A set of dishes

17. What are attendees asked NOT to do?
    (A) Bring their own food
    (B) Charge for alcoholic beverages
    (C) Stay until after dark
    (D) Set off their own fireworks

表を見ながら、次のアナウンスメントを聞いて、質問に対する一番適当と思われる答を (A) (B) (C) (D) から選びなさい。

Announcement 2:

Time	Presentation
9:00	Welcoming
9:30	Home ownership basics
10:00	Financing your dream home
10:30	Break
11:00	Climbing the property ladder
11:30	Question and answer session

18. Who is most likely to attend this seminar?
    (A) People wanting to buy a house.
    (B) People wanting to sell a house.
    (C) People wanting to get a home loan.
    (D) People wanting to rent a house.

19. Look at the graphic. What time will the presentation on financing your dream home now begin?
    (A) 9:45
    (B) 10:00
    (C) 10:15
    (D) 10:30

20. When should attendees ask questions?
    (A) At the end of each presentation
    (B) Immediately following the welcoming session
    (C) During the 15-minute break
    (D) During the question and answer session

READING SECTION (20 questions)

PART 5 Incomplete Sentences （短文穴埋め問題）（2問）

次の文の空欄に一番適当と思われる言葉を (A) (B) (C) (D) から選んで入れなさい。

21. Because Miriam lives so far from the sea, she has always dreamed ------- taking an ocean cruise.
    (A) of
    (B) for
    (C) to
    (D) on

22. Filming for Arlene Ramirez's next film was scheduled to begin shooting next month, but ------- an injury, it has been postponed for two months.
    (A) thanks to
    (B) due to
    (C) resulting from
    (D) as a consequence to

PART 6 Text Completion （長文穴埋め問題）（2 Text × 4問 = 8問）

次の文の空欄に一番適当と思われる答を (A) (B) (C) (D) から選びなさい。

Selection 1: Article

Cheryl Baggins made a name for herself a couple of years ago when she ------- her first novel, *The Smell of Rain*, so it is regrettable that her latest
23.
novel, *Paddles*, does not ------- that momentum. *Paddles* tells the coming-
24.
of-age story of Amanda Lewis, a small-town girl who discovers her ------- of
25.
rowing. Unfortunately, Amanda and many of the book's characters are poorly developed and one-dimensional. Even worse, the ending is totally unrealistic. If you're looking for a young-adult novel to buy your teenager this Christmas, leave this one on the bookstore shelf. -------
26.

23. (A) developed
    (B) devised
    (C) published
    (D) appeared

24. (A) continue
    (B) encourage
    (C) restore
    (D) drive

25. (A) interest
    (B) talent
    (C) care
    (D) love

26. (A) This book is for die-hard Baggins fans only.
    (B) Cheryl Baggins will be reading her new novel at Grand Avenue Books tomorrow evening.
    (C) Cheryl Baggins should give up writing completely.
    (D) This new novel is sure to be a hit with critics and the reading pubic alike.

Selection 2: Article

Perhaps the most annoying aspect of air travel is the long lines at Airport Security. For travelers who are tired of the wait, there is now a __27.__ ! Passengers who sign up for TSA Pre-Check are __28.__ for speedier processing when they arrive at the airport. Interested travelers can apply online. __29.__ must be fingerprinted and agree to a background check and a ten-minute in person interview. Those who receive the special status are issued a Known Traveler Number (KTN), which is added to their ticket. With a KTN, the passengers do not have to remove shoes, belts, or light jackets—and their laptop computers can stay in their cases. Children under 12 can go through the lines with their parents. __30.__ This program has proved to be popular among frequent travelers.

27. (A) response
    (B) solution
    (C) solve
    (D) resolution

28. (A) available
    (B) possible
    (C) eligible
    (D) entitled

29. (A) Applications
    (B) Applying
    (C) Applicators
    (D) Applicants

30. (A) This new service is going a long way toward removing some of the stress of air travel.
    (B) The new service will not make air travel more convenient during peak seasons, however, so it's not as helpful as expected.
    (C) Putting KTN numbers on passports would go against most privacy policies.
    (D) Fingerprinting will soon be made a requirement for all airline passengers entering the country.

PART 7 Reading Comprehension 読解問題（10問）

次の3つの文書を読んで、一番適当と思われる答を (A) (B) (C) (D) から選びなさい。

Selection 1:
Material 1:

E-mail 1
From: Department of Human Resources
To: All Employees
Date: March 31
Subject: New Policy
To All Employees: We are happy to announce the following changes to our sick-leave policy. Beginning April 1st, both sick and vacation time will be combined into one form of leave to be described as Personal Time Off (PTO). Employees may decide for themselves how to use this time, which can be used for sick leave or accumulated as vacation time. PTO also includes maternity leave and leave for family illness or other emergencies. Leave time that employees have already earned will be carried over to the new system and can also be carried over to the next calendar year. Rules about how leave time is acquired will not change. If you have any questions, please contact Human Resources. Sincerely, Richard Pettyworth Head of Human Resources

Material 2:

E-mail 2
From: Michael Preston
To: Department of Human Resources
Date: April 1
Subject: Vacation time
Dear Sir: I have a question regarding the new leave policy. I have been saving my vacation days to take a two-week trip this summer. However, last year, I took some sick time to be with my wife when our child was born. If the different types of leave time are combined into one system, will I be able to save up enough time to take my vacation as planned? Will I still be able to keep the vacation time I now have? Or do I have to start over? Respectfully, Michael Preston

Material 3:

E-mail 3
From: Department of Human Resources
To: Matthew Preston
Date: April 3
Subject: Re: Vacation time
Dear Mr. Preston: As we explained in our memo, sick leave and vacation leave will no longer be counted separately. Since you were specifically saving your vacation time, you will still have that time credited to you, but it will no longer be counted as exclusively vacation time. The time you have saved will be available for multiple uses, including sick leave or parental leave. You will be able to use this leave time at your discretion as you choose, or as necessity dictates. Therefore, you will be able to use your time for your vacation. However, since you used up your sick leave last year, your current account includes only the accumulated vacation time. If you wish to take your vacation as planned, you may not have sufficient time left over to use for other purposes.

31. Who is the first email intended for?
    (A) Employees of the Human Resources Department
    (B) Employees who want to take a vacation
    (C) All employees
    (D) Employees who want to use their sick leave

32. What is the most important change in the new policy?
    (A) There will no longer be different kinds of leave.
    (B) Employees will now be allowed to take maternity leave.
    (C) Employees will no longer be able to change their vacation schedule.
    (D) The process for acquiring leave time has been changed.

33. Why has Mr. Preston been saving his leave time?
    (A) He is planning to take a family leave next year.
    (B) He is planning to take a vacation.
    (C) To make up time for his being sick last year
    (D) He wants to spend time with his new baby.

34. What is Mr. Preston concerned about?
    (A) He will not have enough time to be with his wife when their child is born.
    (B) He will not be able to combine different types of leave.
    (C) He will have to start accumulating vacation time all over.
    (D) He will not be able to take leave the next time he is sick.

35. After reading email 3, how will Mr. Preston probably feel?
    (A) Disappointed that he will not be able to take his vacation.
    (B) Sorry that he took sick leave last year.
    (C) Frustrated that his question was not answered properly.
    (D) Reassured by the Human Resources Department's explanation.

次の3つの文書を読んで、一番適当と思われる答を (A) (B) (C) (D) から選びなさい。

Selection 2:
Material 1: Chat Discussion

> Margaret Choi: Hey, thanks for taking some time out of your lunch break to chat with me about the details of the company quiz night.
> Asiz Rahmaan: No problem! When you suggested it at last week's meeting, I thought it would be a great opportunity to promote team building within the company.
> Margaret Choi: Do you have any ideas for where we should hold it? I was thinking of 29 Mix, but it can be a bit expensive.
> Asiz Rahmaan: True, but it is the closest possible venue to the office. Hmm, how many people are coming?
> Margaret Choi: About 30 in total, so we should take the size of the venue into consideration as well.
> Asiz Rahmaan: In that case, why not have it at Splash? It's not too much farther from the office, plus I think they offer a discount on parties of 15 or more.
> Margaret Choi: Hmm, that could work, then. Can you send me the information? I'll send them an email tonight.

Material 2: Venue Information

SPLASH!
Home to the best drinks in town!

Open: 5P.M. ~ 3A.M., Mon-Sun (closed on Tuesdays and holidays)
Happy Hour: Every day from 5-8.
Drink specials daily!
Great for parties!*

*For parties:
-Minimum of 10 people
-Groups of 30 people and up will receive a 20% discount
-Custom drink/appetizer menus available; please inquire by email
-Happy Hour prices do not apply to group events
parties@splash.com

Material 3:

E-mail
From: Margaret Choi (MargaretC@interlink.com)
To: Splash party (parties@splash.com)
Subject: Quiz night at Splash

To whom it may concern,

My name is Margaret Choi, and I am the director of Human Resources at Interlink Finance Solutions.

My colleagues and I are interested in having a quiz night at your venue, and I would like to arrange a time to use your space. I was thinking Tuesday night, but since you are closed on Tuesdays, I figure we can have it the next day. Since it will be a weeknight, we'd like to begin at around 7 and end at 9. We were expecting a crowd of 30, but one person will not be able to make it due to prior commitments. Even so, would you be willing to let it slide and give us the 20% discount? We'd very much appreciate it. In return, we would be more than willing to publicize your bar by posting pictures of our quiz night on our company's web site.

With regards to the drinks, I was thinking a couple of pints per person of draft beer and a few bottles of wine would be fine. Also, since this will be a quiz night, I was wondering if you had any equipment and supplies we could use, specifically a projector or screen, a speaker, microphone, whiteboards, and markers. If so, could you let us use them? You can include any rental fees for the equipment in our bill.

Regards,
Margaret Choi
Director, Human Resources
Interlink Financial Solutions

36. What seems to be the main reason that Margaret and Asiz are organizing a quiz night?
    (A) To strengthen interpersonal relationships at work
    (B) To give the employees a break
    (C) To test employees' ability to answer general-information questions
    (D) To gather new ideas from employees for team building

37. How many people are required to attend in order for a group to receive a 20% discount at Splash?
    (A) 15 or more
    (B) 19 or more
    (C) 29 or more
    (D) 30 or more

38. What does "let it slide" mean in paragraph 2, line 6 of Margaret Choi's email to Splash?
    (A) overlook it
    (B) discuss it
    (C) negotiate it
    (D) confirm it

39. What does Margaret offer to do for Splash in return for being given the group discount?
    (A) Post pictures of the quiz night on the bar's webpage
    (B) Order her employees to use the bar more often
    (C) Improve the bar's public image through word of mouth
    (D) Post pictures of the bar on her company's website

40. What is the manager of the bar most likely to do next?
    (A) Start setting up for the company's quiz night
    (B) Turn down all of Margaret's requests
    (C) Send Margaret a reply
    (D) Hire extra wait staff to handle such a large group

Unit 6
Careers and Employment

Key Expressions

Step 1　A 欄の語彙に合う訳を B 欄から選びましょう。

A.
1. making ends meet
2. a temporary employee
3. perplexed
4. compliment
5. congratulations
6. promotion
7. boost
8. supervising
9. graphics department
10. fringe benefits

B.
a. 監督する；指揮する
b. デザイン部
c. 昇進；昇級
d. おめでとう
e. 臨時雇用社員
f. 付加給与
g. 範囲内でやりくりする
h. 褒め言葉
i. 当惑した；混乱した
j. 増額

Dialog: Guess What!?

Step 2　Dialog の中の空白に Key Expressions から当てはまる言葉を選びましょう。必要ならば語形を変えて入れてください。

Gary is telling Beth about his new position at his company.

Gary: Guess what, Beth! I got a (A) (　　　　)!

Beth: Wow, really? So, does that mean you're leaving the (B) (　　　　)?

Gary: Not at all. I'm going to be the assistant manager. Beth, why are you looking at me like that? This is great news.

Beth: I'm actually feeling kind of (C) (　　　　). I thought you liked your job.

Gary: I do! I love it! I mean, drawing all day has always been my life's goal. But this will give me a big (D) (　　　　) in pay, and you know I'm having a hard time (E) (　　　　) on what they pay me now since I'm only (F) (　　　　). But now I'll have a regular, full-time salary with all the (G) (　　　　). And security!

Beth: I'm very happy for you, but gee, Gary, you're such a great artist. When are you going to have the time and energy to draw if you're (H) (　　　　) the other artists all day?

Gary: That, of course, is a bit of a drawback. But anyway, thanks for the (I) (　　　　) on my talent. I guess I'll just have to take my sketch book with me on my lunch break. And my weekends are free! By the way, I have some new cartoons. I'll send you some.

Beth: Thanks, and, oh, I almost forgot (J) (　　　　)!

Dialog Comprehension

Step 3　Dialog に関する次の質問に答えましょう。

1. How does Beth feel about Gary's news?
   (A) She is relieved that he will not have to draw anymore.
   (B) She is a little worried that he will miss doing his artwork.
   (C) She is proud of him for taking on more responsibility.

2. What is Gary's current job?
   (A) He's a part-time graphic artist.
   (B) He's an assistant manager.
   (C) He supervises other artists.

LISTENING SECTION

PART 1 Photographs（写真描写問題）（2問）

文を聞いて写真と一番一致するものを (A) (B) (C) (D) から選びなさい。

1. (A) (B) (C) (D)

2. (A) (B) (C) (D)

PART 2 Question-Response （応答問題）（3問）

質問または文を聞いて、一番適当と思われる応答を (A) (B) (C) から選びなさい。

1. (A) (B) (C) 2. (A) (B) (C) 3. (A) (B) (C)

PART 3 Conversation （会話問題）（3問）

会話文を聞いて質問に対する一番適当と思われる答えを (A) (B) (C) (D) から選びなさい。

Professional Development Workshops	Tuesday, May 2
7:30 – 9:00 a.m.	How to Deal with Difficult People
7:45 – 9:15 a.m.	Presentation Skills
9:00 – 10:30 a.m.	Planning Your Retirement
1:00 – 2:30 p.m.	New Technology

1. Which seminar did Jeff sign up for?
   (A) How to Deal with Difficult People
   (B) Presentation Skills
   (C) Planning Your Retirement
   (D) New Technology

2. Look at the graphic. What time will the seminar that Diane is interested in be held?
   (A) 7:30 – 9:00 a.m.
   (B) 7:45 – 9:15 a.m.
   (C) 9:00 – 10:30 a.m.
   (D) 1:00 – 2:30 p.m.

3. What can we infer about both Jeff and Diane?
   (A) They are difficult to get along with.
   (B) They are not early risers.
   (C) They are nearing retirement age.
   (D) They are conducting the seminars.

PART 4 Talks （説明文問題）（3問）

次のアナウンスメントを聞いて、質問に対する一番適当と思われる答を (A) (B) (C) (D) から選びなさい。

1. What is the topic of this meeting?
   (A) How to organize the seating arrangements
   (B) Planning a welcoming party for Model Sound Corporation
   (C) Discussing the effects of the big change that is happening to the company
   (D) To fill in the gaps in the organizational chart

2. What does the announcer ask the audience to do first of all?
   (A) Move to the front of the auditorium so they can hear and see better
   (B) Stay in their seats until the talk ends
   (C) Copy the organizational chart on the screen onto the paper in their folders
   (D) Move to the empty seats in the center to make room for more participants

3. When will the merger take place?
   (A) This coming July
   (B) July next year
   (C) Last July
   (D) Next week

TOEIC のための満点アプリ
PART 2 Question-Response 応答問題

質問も選択肢もテストブックに印刷されていませんから、しっかり集中して聞くことが大切です。全部で 25 問です。

PART 2 の質問文は次の三種類。そのパターンを覚えよう！

Point 1- STATEMENT-RESPONESE 平叙文 – 応答
Point 2- YES, NO で答える質問
Point 3- WH の疑問詞 what, who, which, when, where, how から始まる質問

▶ **STATEMENT-RESPONESE　あなたならどう答えますか？**

日常会話や、ビジネスシーンで、一番私達 Non-native が苦労するのは、相手の言ったことに対して、とっさにコメントを返すということではないでしょうか。
PART 2 では、25 問中 5 問から 8 問がこのステートメント（平叙文）—応答に関する出題。TOEIC 750 点以上を目指す人にとっては落とせないところです。また、"You speak good English!" "Thanks." などと単純な文ではなく、"Well, I don't speak as well as I should." 「もっと話せなければいけないんですけどね。」などと、ちょっとひねった答えが正解になっています。

READING SECTION

Grammar Points
TOEIC 頻出ポイント：Future Tense　未来形のさまざまな表現

未来形の表現はビジネスや日常のことを話すのにいちばん使われる頻度が高い文型の一つです。未来のことを話すのによく使われる型は will + 動詞の原形 (e.g. **I will make, do** など) ですが、これだけではなく、他にも色々な表現の仕方があります。

▶ Point 1　be going to + 動詞の原形

考えて決めたことに対して使います。

a. **I'm going to apply** for a job as a flight attendant.

見たり、聞いたり、感じたりしたことから、次に起こることを予測します。

b. Be careful! **The curtain is going to catch fire**.

▶ Point 2　will + 動詞の原形

公的なアナウンスメントに使われます。

c. Flight 306 **will arrive** at Gate 12.

突然の出来事に対してとっさに反応するときに使われます。

d. A: Could someone please erase the board?　B: **I'll do** it!

when, if, after を伴う文に使われます。*

e. After I eat dinner, I **will help** you with your homework.

▶ Point 3　be + ~ing　決定した予定について話すとき使います。

f. **I'm having** lunch with Cathy tomorrow.

▶ Point 4　will be + ~ing　未来のある時点でしていることを表現します。

g. **I'll be sleeping** when you get home, so please come in quietly.

▶ Point 5　will have + 過去分詞　二つの時の関係を表します。

h. I'm going to miss my flight. By the time I **get** to the airport, the plane **will have left**.*

* しかし when, if, after, by the time などの節の中では will, be going to, have+ 過去分詞などの分詞形は使えません。次の文を比べて下さい。

○ **By the tIme I get** to the airport, the plane will have left.
× **By the time I will ge**t to the airport, the plane will have left.

Grammar Quiz (5問)

次の文を読んで、一番適当と思われる語を選びなさい。

1. Shh! Be quiet! The movie ------- now.
   - (A) has been starting
   - (B) starts
   - (C) is going to start
   - (D) will starting

2. A: Please say hello to your wife for me.
   B: Thanks, -------.
   - (A) I am
   - (B) I will
   - (C) I'm going to
   - (D) I will be

3. By the time you ------- this postcard, I will have moved on to Denmark.
   - (A) receive
   - (B) received
   - (C) will receive
   - (D) had received

4. ------- Don for coffee at 3:00. Can you join us?
   - (A) I'm meeting
   - (B) I will have met
   - (C) I met
   - (D) I meet

5. When you get to the restaurant tonight, look for us. We ------- by the window.
   - (A) sit
   - (B) will be sitting
   - (C) sat
   - (D) are sitting

PART 5 Incomplete Sentences（短文穴埋め問題）（2問）

次の文の空欄に一番適当と思われる答を (A) (B) (C) (D) から選びなさい。

1. It's raining now, but I'm going to get in the car and drive to the beach anyway. It's a 20-minute drive, so I'm hoping that by the time I get there, the rain -------.
   (A) stopped
   (B) stops
   (C) will stop
   (D) will have stopped

2. If you try calling me within the next hour, I might not answer because -------.
   (A) I'm going to drive
   (B) I'll drive
   (C) I'll be driving
   (D) I will have driven

PART 6 Text Completion（長文穴埋め問題）（4問）

次の文の4つの空欄に一番適当と思われる答を (A) (B) (C) (D) から選びなさい。

Text: Document

ChoreHorse is an example of a company in the new "sharing" economy that is emerging in the United States. Clients of ChoreHorse hire an ordinary person to come to their house to help with all sorts of ordinary household tasks. -------. Or, you may hire me to look after your dog while you are out of town. ChoreHorse employees check a website to see what ------- clients want done, and then sign up for a job if they have the skills to do it. Employees work as much or as little -------. Economists predict that the new sharing economy ------- to grow as traditional jobs become increasingly scarce.

1. (A) Of course, it depends on what kind of chores you like to do.
   (B) For example, I might hire you to frame my pictures and put them up on the wall.
   (C) I could share a house with you so that we can split the household expenses.
   (D) Most of the tasks involve skills that do not require professional training.

2. (A) tasks
   (B) number
   (C) equipment
   (D) finances

3. (A) as possible
   (B) that they can
   (C) often as necessary
   (D) as they want

4. (A) is continuing
   (B) will continue
   (C) continues
   (D) continued

PART 7 Reading Comprehension (読解問題)（5問）

次の3つの文書を読んで、一番適当と思われる答を (A) (B) (C) (D) から選びなさい。

Material 1: Newspaper Article

> Castle Hotel, which has been struggling financially for the past three years, has announced its acquisition by Great Resort Holdings. Under the new ownership, all of the hotel's 157 rooms will be remodeled and updated, and its other amenities and services will be improved and expanded. Although the room staff will be retained, Great Resort plans to bring in new personnel at the management level. The company will also be hiring locally to fill positions at the front desk, lobby bar/lounge, gift shop, pool, and golf course—and at a brand-new 4-star restaurant. "This is very good news for our lagging economy," says Maxine Collins, city manager of Beachville. According to Great Resort Vice-President of Operations, Bob Gall, openings for local hires will be posted in January on the company's website: www.grandresort.com. The hotel will be closed from November to February for renovations. A grand opening is planned for early March.

Material 2:

E-mail 1
To: Rachel Taylor
From: Kimberly Farr
Subject: Castle Hotel employment
Date: September 29
Dear Ms. Taylor: I saw an article in yesterday's Beachville Times about job openings for Castle Hotel. I am very much interested in managing your gift shop. I opened the "Cutest Gift Shop" in the neighboring town of Shoreline fourteen years ago and have managed the shop myself ever since. I have always wanted to relocate to Beachville, and I think that this may be my big chance. I have enclosed my resume and references. I hope to hear from you soon. Thank you very much. Sincerely, Kimberly Farr

Material 3:

E-mail 2
To: Kimberly Farr
From: Rachel Taylor
Subject: Re: Castle Hotel Employment
Date: October 15

Dear Ms. Farr:

Thank you for your inquiry regarding a position at the Castle Hotel gift shop. As the article you read mentioned, our job listings will be posted in January. Until then, it is too early to say what positions will be listed for the gift shop. In general, our management positions will be filled internally by Great Resort Holdings via transfers from other hotels in our company. Exceptions may be made, however, for highly qualified local applicants. Please visit our website again in January for a complete listing of new positions. Again, thank you for your interest in Castle Hotel.

Rachel Taylor
Personnel Director

1. What changes are planned for Castle Hotel?
   (A) New room staff, a new restaurant, and a golf course
   (B) Building expansion, new front-desk personnel, and a new name
   (C) A new pool, a change in personnel, and local staff hiring
   (D) New management, renovations, and expanded services

2. What is NOT mentioned in the article?
   (A) The reason for Castle Hotel's financial struggles
   (B) When a list of job openings will be posted
   (C) Beachville's current economic condition
   (D) The amenities and services the hotel will offer

3. Which of the following does Ms. Farr emphasize about her qualifications for the position?
   (A) Her work experience
   (B) Her desire to relocate to Beachville
   (C) Her familiarity with the Castle Hotel
   (D) Her desire to sell her gift shop

4. Which of the following is mentioned in both Ms. Taylor's email and in the newspaper article?
    (A) The gift shop manager's position is to be filled through an internal transfer.
    (B) Job listings will not be posted until January.
    (C) Most management jobs will be filled locally.
    (D) Castle Hotel will be closed until early March.

5. What does Ms. Taylor's email imply?
    (A) The position of gift shop manager has already been filled.
    (B) Ms. Farr has no chance of getting a job at Castle Hotel.
    (C) Ms. Farr's inquiry has been made too soon for Ms. Taylor to answer it.
    (D) Ms. Taylor feels that Ms. Farr is over-qualified for the job.

Unit 7
Advertisements and Sales Campaign

Key Expressions

Step 1　A 欄の語彙に合う訳を B 欄から選びましょう。

A. 1. niche
   2. post
   3. publish
   4. keep track
   5. amazing
   6. linked
   7. research
   8. subscription
   9. following

B. a. 出版する
   b. すごい；素晴らしい
   c. 調査
   d. 定期購読
   e. （ネット上で）接続された
   f. 支持者；ファン
   g. 発表する；掲載する
   h. 追跡調査する；記録をつける
   i. 自分の得意分野

Dialog: Publish or Perish?

Step 2　Dialog の中の空白に Key Expressions から当てはまる言葉を選びましょう。必要ならば語形を変えて入れてください。

Cindy is giving Kevin some advice on how to sell a story he has written.

Kevin: So, Cindy, what did you think of my short story? Did you read it?

Cindy: Yes, I did. I thought it had some excellent things going for it. But I'm afraid the writing is not quite up to the quality of writing that we (A) (　　　) here. You should try to market your stories online.

Kevin: Really? Sell my stories online? How? To whom?

Cindy: I can show you how because as a matter of fact, I sell my short stories online. I have a website (B) (　　　) to PayPal. I write stories and (C) (　　　) them on the website. Customers can buy a (D) (　　　) to my stories and get a new story every month. Or they can buy my stories one at a time.

Kevin: How will I know what people want to read and how to price the stories?

Cindy: Easy. You do a little (E) (　　　). You start with a variety of stories—mysteries, romances, adventure tales—and you offer them free of charge at first. Then you (F) (　　　) of the number of hits you get. That's how you find out what's popular out there. That's going to be what is called your (G) (　　　). You keep writing the stories that people like best, and once you have developed a

79

loyal (H) (　　　　　), you start charging for your stories. Then, if you're lucky, your readers will be willing to pay the price.
Kevin: That's (I) (　　　　　). So, what do your customers like to read?
Cindy: Romantic fantasies about rock stars.
Kevin: You've got to be kidding!

Dialog Comprehension

Step 3　Dialog に関する次の質問に答えましょう。

1. What does Cindy think Kevin should do?
   (A) Buy Cindy's stories
   (B) Sell his stories online
   (C) Help her market her stories

2. Which of the following best represents the order of the steps of the process that Cindy describes?
   (A) Offer a free product, develop a loyal customer base, sell the product
   (B) Develop a loyal customer base, offer a free product, sell the product
   (C) Sell a product, develop a loyal customer base, offer a free product

LISTENING SECTION

PART 1 Photographs（写真描写問題）（2問）

文を聞いて写真と一番一致するものを (A) (B) (C) (D) から選びなさい。

1. (A) (B) (C) (D)

2. (A) (B) (C) (D)

Unit 7

PART 2 Question-Response（応答問題）（3問）

質問または文を聞いて、一番適当と思われる応答を (A) (B) (C) から選びなさい。

1. (A) (B) (C)   2. (A) (B) (C)   3. (A) (B) (C)

PART 3 Conversation（会話問題）（3問）

会話文を聞いて質問に対する一番適当と思われる答えを (A) (B) (C) (D) から選びなさい。

> **Slide 7: Slogans**
>   A good slogan…
> • is memorable
> • is catchy
> • has product identification

1. Look at the slide. Which characteristic of a good slogan does John's slogan have?
   (A) None of them
   (B) Memorable
   (C) Catchy
   (D) Has product identification

2. What will the new slogan be?
   (A) "Enjoy a relaxing moment with a cup of fresh-brewed Foxy coffee."
   (B) "Be Foxy."
   (C) "That Foxy morning aroma"
   (D) "Morning aroma"

3. What will they do next?
   (A) Have a cup of coffee
   (B) Go to sleep
   (C) Come up with more slogans
   (D) Go out somewhere for breakfast

PART 4 Talks（説明文問題）（3問）

次のアナウンスメントを聞いて、質問に対する一番適当と思われる答を (A) (B) (C) (D) から選びなさい。

1. Where do you wear the Walk-o-Meter?
    (A) Around your neck
    (B) On your belt
    (C) On your wrist
    (D) On your ankle

2. Why does the Walk-o-Meter have such a long battery life?
    (A) It has special features that save the battery.
    (B) It keeps things simple.
    (C) It has a self-charging battery.
    (D) It is small and lightweight.

3. Which is NOT a feature of the Walk-o-Meter?
    (A) It is surprisingly expensive.
    (B) It connects with your smartphone.
    (C) It records your heart rate.
    (D) It counts your steps.

TOEIC のための満点アプリ
PART 3 Conversations 会話問題

A-B-A-B, A-B-A-B-A などの二人の会話を聞き、それに対する質問が3問あります。PART 2と違って、質問はテストブックにプリントされています。全部で39問です。700点以上目指すなら、この PART 3 では得点75%以上が望ましいです。

会話自体はそれほど難解な語彙はありませんが、ビジネス関連の会話や native な表現も多いので、まだビジネス経験のない学生諸君にとってはある意味では PART 4 Announcements より、聞き取りにくいパートかもしれません。

対策としては、しっかり CD を聞きながら shadowing* をするのが効果的です。
*shadowing ... 5ページ「TOEIC の得点を上げ、英語を身につけるための学習法」参照。

▶まずは質問を読もう
会話文から始まる前に必ず質問のキーワードを scanning しておきましょう。
PART 3 ではしっかり質問のキーワードを目でにらみながら会話文を耳から聞くという2次元的なアプローチが必要になります。

READING SECTION

Grammar Points
TOEIC 頻出ポイント：Subject-Verb Agreement　主語と動詞の関係

Unit 5 では**冠詞と数量詞** Articles and Quantifiers について学びましたが、長い文の中で、どれが主語かを見極めて、それを離れたところにある動詞につなぐ出題は TOEIC, PART 5 PART 6 の頻出ポイントです。主語が単数形か複数形かによって、動詞の形が違うのは、日本語には無い観念なので、私たちにとってはかなり苦手の分野になります。
次のいくつかの注意ポイントを覚えましょう。

▶ **Point 1　単数複数に関する頻出ポイント**

a. **one of, none of** につく動詞は単数扱い
   One of my friends (~~are~~ / **is**) helping me move into my new apartment.

b. テストでは逆に動詞から類推させる問題もある。動詞が複数を表すときは主語も複数を表す **a few** が正解。
   (~~One~~ / **A few**) of the classrooms have air conditioning.

c. **almost all of** + the students（可算名詞複数形）の形。Almost students と間違える人がとても多いので注意。
   (~~Almost~~ / **Almost all of**) the flights were delayed because of the bad weather.

d. All に関するポイント。**all of** + the information（不可算名詞）につく動詞は単数扱い。
   All of the furniture in the storage room (**needs** / ~~need~~) to be repaired.

e. All に関するポイント。**all of** + the books（可算名詞）につく動詞は複数扱い。
   All of the employees on the third floor (~~is~~ / **are**) required to attend the meeting.

▶ **Point 2　Addressing Public（一般的な呼びかけ）**

f. 特別のグループでなく一般に向けて「学生諸君；皆さん」呼び掛けるときは **all students** となる。
   Attention (**all shoppers** / ~~all of the shoppers~~)! Vitamin supplements are 15% off today.

▶ **Point 3　each, every, は単数扱い**

g. Each cookie (**is** / ~~are~~) hand-dipped in chocolate and individually wrapped.

h. Make sure that every child (**has** / ~~have~~) a pencil and a piece of paper.

Grammar Quiz (5問)

次の文を読んで、一番適当と思われる語を選びなさい。

1. Timmy ate ------- his dinner, and he put the rest of it in a small box away in the refrigerator.
   (A) almost
   (B) almost of
   (C) almost all of
   (D) all most

2. Each ------- important to our business.
   (A) customer is
   (B) customer are
   (C) customers was
   (D) customers are

3. All ------- in my family ------- blue eyes.
   (A) of girls ... have
   (B) of girls ... has
   (C) of the girls ... have
   (D) of the girls ... has

4. Your attention, please. All ------- should proceed to Gate 13B.
   (A) passengers
   (B) passenger
   (C) of passengers
   (D) the passengers

5. Every ------- that stealing is wrong.
   (A) children know
   (B) child know
   (C) children knows
   (D) child knows

PART 5 Incomplete Sentences (短文穴埋め問題) (2問)

次の文の空欄に一番適当と思われる答を (A) (B) (C) (D) から選びなさい。

1. A few ------- sitting on the steps of the library checking their phones.
   (A) students were
   (B) student was
   (C) students was
   (D) student were

2. Each ------- without rain ------- the worry that we are headed into a serious drought.
   (A) days ... increase
   (B) day ... increases
   (C) days ... increases
   (D) day ... increase

PART 6 Text Completion （長文穴埋め問題）（4問）

次の文の4つの空欄に一番適当と思われる答を (A) (B) (C) (D) から選びなさい。

Text: Article

One of the most important steps for a group when setting up a non-profit organization ------- the creation of the donation page on your website. Here are some of the guidelines that commercial websites use. First, try to limit your donation page to only one page. ------- Second, give your donors choices in the method of payment. Include at least three options. Most people will want to pay by credit card, so, of course, you must have that option. But you should also ------- PayPal as an electronic-check option. Finally, give donors a choice ------- monthly donations and one-time donations. A good donor website can make a big difference in how much you receive in donations.

1. (A) are
   (B) is
   (C) was
   (D) were

2. (A) There are several other payment options available.
   (B) Commercial web pages are much more complex than charity websites.
   (C) Keep it as short and simple as you can.
   (D) One page is too short for all of the information that needs to be included.

3. (A) include
   (B) includes
   (C) including
   (D) included

4. (A) between
   (B) for
   (C) about
   (D) among

PART 7 Reading Comprehension （読解問題）（5 問）

次の 3 つの文書を読んで、一番適当と思われる答を (A) (B) (C) (D) から選びなさい。

Material 1:

E-mail 1
To: All Store Managers
From: Headquarters
Subject: Promotional Event
Date: April 3
MaxOut Super Stores will soon unveil a one-week promotional event designed to encourage our customers to choose the MaxOut credit card when they make their purchases. Up until now, there has been no incentive for customers to use their MaxOut credit card, even if they have one, so many customers have been using whatever credit card they habitually use for purchases. The result is that MaxOut Super Stores has seen losses in the form of fees charged to us by certain credit-card companies. To support this promotional event, sales associates will receive a bonus for each new MaxOut credit-card account they open.

Material 2:

E-mail 2
To: All Sales Associates
From: MaxOut Super Stores – Prince Mall
Subject: Promotional Event Mandatory Meeting
Date: April 15
Every sales associate is required to attend one of three mandatory meetings in preparation for our upcoming promotional event. All meetings will take place in the Plumeria Room. Please choose one of the three meeting times. Reply to this message by April 20 with your name, employee number, and the date of the meeting you will attend. You will receive a confirmation number by return. Please choose one: April 27   8:00 – 9:00 A.M. April 28   12:00 – 1:00 P.M. April 29   2:00 – 3:00 P.M. If you are unable to attend at any of these times, contact your immediate supervisor as soon as possible. Shirley Ochikoff Store Manager

Unit 7

Material 3: Advertisement

> **Super Summer Savings at MaxOut! June 15 – 22!**
> One whole week of super-duper savings! Get a 10% discount off your purchases every time you use your MaxOut card! Don't have a MaxOut card yet? No problem! To join the MaxOut family, just bring your purchases up to any check-out station. Open a new account with us right there on the spot. Use your new MaxOut card that very day, and get a super 20% discount on your purchase! Come right back the very next day for your 10% discount! And the next day!

1. Why haven't customers been using their MaxOut card?
   - (A) They don't like the design.
   - (B) There is no advantage to using it.
   - (C) Opening an account takes too much time.
   - (D) The store charges a fee for using it.

2. The word "incentive" in E-mail 1, line 3, is closest in meaning to which word?
   - (A) motivation
   - (B) excuse
   - (C) trouble
   - (D) function

3. What is the purpose of the meeting in the Plumeria Room?
   - (A) To discuss the store's financial problems
   - (B) To reward sales associates who have made the most sales
   - (C) To explain the promotional event to sales associates
   - (D) To gather ideas for the design of the new credit card

4. Who is the ad intended for?
   - (A) Only regular MaxOut customers
   - (B) Only customers who already have a MaxOut card
   - (C) People who have never shopped at MaxOut
   - (D) Regular MaxOut customers as well as newcomers

5. Where does the ad say that can customers open a new MaxOut account?
   - (A) Online
   - (B) At the nearest bank
   - (C) At the store
   - (D) Over the phone

Unit 8
Communications

Key Expressions

Step 1　A欄の語彙に合う訳をB欄から選びましょう。

A.
1. version
2. awesome
3. operating system
4. feature
5. come by
6. get used to
7. break into
8. extras
9. compatible

B.
a. 侵入する
b. 〜に慣れる
c. 互換性のある
d. おまけ；追加
e. 版；型
f. 素晴らしい
g. 基本ソフト
h. 特徴；機能
i. 寄ってみる

Dialog: Upgrading the System

Step 2　Dialog の中の空白に Key Expressions から当てはまる言葉を選びましょう。必要ならば語形を変えて入れてください。

Jim and Pat are in the office discussing a computer problem.

Pat: Hi, Jim. While you were out, I fixed the problem you were having with your computer this morning.

Jim: Oh, great. Thanks a lot, Pat. What was wrong with it?

Pat: Nothing, really. All I did was upgrade your (A) (　　　　　). You were using an older (B) (　　　　　), and as time goes by, there's less and less (C) (　　　　　) software out there for it. But why were you still using Doorways 7? Everyone was supposed to upgrade to Doorways 8 months ago.

Jim: I've tried using 8 on Gary's computer, but it's just too hard for me to figure out and use.

Pat: It's not harder, Jim. It's just different. Keep at it and you'll (D) (　　　　　) it, I'm sure. And anyway, it has some (E) (　　　　　) new stuff.

Jim: Well, I still don't see why it was so important for us to upgrade. I don't really care about any of those fancy (F) (　　　　　), like games and videos.

Pat: The main reason for the upgrade was that version 8 has new security (G) (　　　). That means it will be harder for anyone to (H) (　　　) your computer. Having everyone on 8 protects the whole company. You see what I mean, right?

Jim: Sure, but why didn't they tell us that in the first place?

Pat: I guess that would have made things easier. Listen, would you like me to (I) (　　　) later and help you get started?

Jim: That would be nice, Pat. I'll be here until 5:00.

Pat: Excellent. See you later, then.

Dialog Comprehension

Step 3　Dialog に関する次の質問に答えましょう。

1. What was the problem with Jim's computer?
   (A) Its operating system was too hard to learn.
   (B) Its operating system needed to be upgraded.
   (C) Someone had broken into it.

2. Why does the company want everyone to upgrade to Doorways 8?
   (A) Doorways 8 has a better security system.
   (B) Doorways 7 needs too many repairs.
   (C) Too many employees were wasting time playing games on Doorways 7.

LISTENING SECTION

PART 1 Photographs（写真描写問題）（2問）

文を聞いて写真と一番一致するものを (A) (B) (C) (D) から選びなさい。

1. (A) (B) (C) (D)

2. (A) (B) (C) (D)

PART 2 Question-Response （応答問題）（3問）

質問または文を聞いて、一番適当と思われる応答を (A) (B) (C) から選びなさい。

1. (A) (B) (C)   2. (A) (B) (C)   3. (A) (B) (C)

PART 3 Conversation （会話問題）（3問）

会話文を聞いて質問に対する一番適当と思われる答えを (A) (B) (C) (D) から選びなさい。

June Events	
Wed. June 7	Neighborhood watch meeting
Sat. June 10	Bingo night
Wed. June 14	Neighborhood board meeting
Sat. June 25	Picnic

1. What was the purpose of the man's phone call?
   (A) To re-schedule an event
   (B) To invite the woman to the neighborhood picnic
   (C) To tell the woman about a mistake she had made
   (D) To change the time and location of the picnic

2. What, most likely, is the man and woman's relationship?
   (A) They are neighborhood board members.
   (B) They work for the same company.
   (C) They write for the same newspaper.
   (D) The man is the woman's boss.

3. Look at the calendar of June Events. What event will the man and woman see each other at next?
   (A) The neighborhood watch meeting
   (B) Bingo night
   (C) The neighborhood board meeting
   (D) The picnic

PART 4 Talks （説明文問題）（3問） 53

次のアナウンスメントを聞いて、質問に対する一番適当と思われる答を (A) (B) (C) (D) から選びなさい。

1. Who is this announcement intended for?
    (A) Airline personnel
    (B) All passengers who have tickets for Flight 242
    (C) All passengers already on board the plane
    (D) Passengers just arriving from Anchorage

2. What should passengers do first?
    (A) Board the next flight to Anchorage
    (B) Get their hotel and meal vouchers
    (C) Go to the customer hospitality desk
    (D) Go to Gate 57 to rebook their flights

3. What do passengers need to show at the hospitality desk?
    (A) Their I.D. and boarding pass
    (B) Their passport and ticket for Flight 242
    (C) Their ticket for Flight 242 and vouchers for food and accommodation
    (D) Their boarding pass and a credit card

READING SECTION

Grammar Points
TOEIC 頻出のポイント：TO+Verb vs Verb+ING　TO をとる動詞と ING をとる動詞

英語では動詞の次にまた動詞を組んで使うことが多いのです。その時 2 つめの動詞は動名詞 (~ing) または不定詞 (to+verb) の形のどちらかの形をとります。TOEC での頻出ポイントの一つです。出題頻度の多い動詞について覚えましょう。

▶ Point 1　~ing が付く動詞

admit, avoid, appreciate, consider, delay, deny, dislike, finish, give up, go on, (can't) help, insist on, practice, mind, miss, suggest, etc.

a. My boss usually finishes **eating** lunch by around 1:00.
b. Sam delayed **going** to college so that he could work for a year.
c. I hope you don't mind my **asking** so many questions.（動名詞の前に「誰が」を入れた形）

▶ Point 2　to が付く動詞

agree, ask, choose, decide, expect, fail, help, hope, intend

d. The board members agreed **to meet** every Tuesday.
e. My colleague asked me **to check** her report.
f. Jeff failed **to inform** his supervisor about his plans.

▶ Point 3　~ing が付くか to が付くかで意味が変わる動詞

remember, stop, try

g. I **remember** signing the documents last month.「したことを覚えている」
h. Please **remember** to lock the door when you leave.「することを忘れないで」
i. It's a good thing that you finally **stopped** smoking.「するのをやめた」
j. Let's work for two hours and then **stop** to get a snack.「するために立ち止まった」

▶ Point 4　よく間違って to をつけられる動詞

demand, suggest, recommend, request などは特殊な文型：<u>demand + (that) + 主語 + 動詞の原形</u>になります。

k. Jen's supervisor **recommended that** she apply for the promotion.
　(× recommended her to)
l. The customers **requested that** the store provide restrooms.
　(× requested the store to)

Grammar Quiz (5問)

次の文を読んで、一番適当と思われる語を選びなさい。

1. Please stop ------- everybody, and listen!
   (A) to talk
   (B) me to talk
   (C) my talking
   (D) talking

2. I really appreciated ------- me the other day.
   (A) your helping
   (B) your help
   (C) your to help
   (D) you to help

3. My department chief demands ------- at work ten minutes early every day.
   (A) me arriving
   (B) me to arrive
   (C) that I arrive
   (D) my arriving

4. How did you get ------- off the TV?
   (A) the children turned
   (B) the children to turn
   (C) the children for turning
   (D) the children's turning

5. John expects ------- a raise next year.
   (A) to get
   (B) getting
   (C) to getting
   (D) that he gets

PART 5 Incomplete Sentences (短文穴埋め問題) (2問)

次の文の空欄に一番適当と思われる答を (A) (B) (C) (D) から選びなさい。

1. If you avoid ------- to work during rush hour, you can get to the office in fifteen minutes instead of forty-five.
    (A) to drive
    (B) driving
    (C) yourself to drive
    (D) drive

2. I suggest ------- a flight before June 1 in order to get a better price.
    (A) you to book
    (B) you booking
    (C) to book you
    (D) that you book

PART 6 Text Completion (長文穴埋め問題) (4問)

次の文の4つの空欄に一番適当と思われる答を (A) (B) (C) (D) から選びなさい。

Text: Advertisement

Did you know that you can now read the *Daily News* online? The e-Edition looks exactly like a print newspaper. You can turn the pages, zoom in and enlarge articles and photos, and ------- print them out. A great feature that you
1.
don't get with the print edition is that you can ------- the whole paper in just a
2.
few seconds. And you can read the e-Edition anywhere! Read it at home or access it ------- your mobile device. Subscribe to the e-Edition now! ------- To
3.   4.
subscribe, you will need to install Internet Player. If you need assistance, visit the Internet Player Installation Help Site.

1. (A) however
   (B) yet
   (C) still
   (D) even

2. (A) searching
   (B) search
   (C) to search
   (D) be searching

3. (A) on
   (B) at
   (C) in
   (D) for

4. (A) You can also buy the print edition at any newsstand.
   (B) Download the e-Edition to your mobile device.
   (C) It's your last chance.
   (D) We're offering a special sign-up rate of only $12.95 a month or $120.00 a year.

PART 7 Reading Comprehension (読解問題) (5問)

次の3つの文書を読んで、一番適当と思われる答を (A) (B) (C) (D) から選びなさい。

Material 1:

E-mail 1
To: Scott, Cory
From: Andrea
Subject: video conference rehearsal
Date: Oct. 1

Hi, all,
Our department is planning to hold a mandatory technical rehearsal before the October 18 video conference with Sassy Fashions. The reason—the need—for the rehearsal is that we have a brand-new video-conferencing unit that none of us has ever used before. Basically, we are going to run through the set-up and make sure the room (C-129) has everything we need. It shouldn't take more than 30 minutes of everyone's time. Since Molly is the most tech-savvy among us, I've asked her when she will be available, and she's named the times below. Everyone, please get back to me ASAP and let me know which of these times works for you.

    Molly's available times:
    Mon. Oct 8   10:30
    Tues. Oct. 9   12:15
    Thurs. Oct. 11   2:45
    in Room C-129

Thanks,
Andrea

Material 2:

E-mail 2
To: Andrea, Scott, Cory
From: Molly
Subject: video conference rehearsal
Date: Oct. 5

Dear all,

  I'm so sorry to tell you that something has come up, and I will not be able to attend the scheduled technical rehearsal after all. I have attached some instructions in what I hope is plain English for how to set up the new video-conferencing unit because I know how frustrating it can be to try and find what you're looking for in those manuals. So, please read the attachment before you try anything else. Also, before Thursday's rehearsal, try to become familiar with the manual so that you will at least know where to look if you need to troubleshoot. The unit—with the manual—is still in its unopened box. I've locked it away in the bottom drawer of the file cabinet in the meeting room. You all know where the key is hidden. Cory, will you please take charge?

  I will be back in the office on October 15. If there are any unresolved issues, we can take those up then. And I will be arriving in the conference room 30 minutes early on the 18th to help set up. Keep in touch by email, and please keep everyone's names in this circular.

Molly

Material 3: E-mail attachment

How to Start Your Video Conference

1. Turn on the wall switch. Turn on the TV screen and the camera on/off switch to "ON."

2. Place the microphone in a position where it will pick up the voices of everyone in the room. Try to put the microphone cord in a place where people are not going to walk or trip over it. Tape the cord down with masking tape in several places if this is not possible.

3. Once the unit is powered up, you might see a message on the screen that says, "No video input." This message will only be displayed for a short time. But if it does not go away within a few minutes, make sure you don't press any of the buttons on the remote control until you have read the troubleshooting section in the manual.

4. The screen should then be displayed. There will be a short initialization period while the unit registers on the network, and then it will be available to use.

Unit 8

1. Why is Molly's schedule so important?
   (A) Because she is the most dependable member of the group.
   (B) Because she is the sales rep who is visiting from Sassy Fashions.
   (C) Because she works for the company that makes the video conferencing unit.
   (D) Because they need her expertise to learn how to use the new unit.

2. When will the technical rehearsal be held?
   (A) October 8
   (B) October 9
   (C) October 11
   (D) October 18

3. What is the main message of Molly's email?
   (A) She will miss the technical rehearsal.
   (B) She will miss the video conference.
   (C) She wants Cory to be in charge of the technical rehearsal.
   (D) She would like everyone to read the manual before the video conference.

4. What should they do with the microphone?
   (A) Tape it down with masking tape in several places.
   (B) Put it where everyone can be heard.
   (C) Walk around it if it isn't possible to step over it.
   (D) Pass it around to everyone in the room.

5. In which of these situations should they look at the relevant troubleshooting section?
   (A) As soon as they power up the unit.
   (B) After the screen is displayed.
   (C) When the initialization period registers the unit on the network.
   (D) If the "No video input" message does not disappear within a few minutes.

97

Unit 9
Complaints and Troubleshooting

Key Expressions

Step 1　A欄の語彙に合う訳をB欄から選びましょう。

A.
1. press coverage
2. failure
3. project (v)
4. agenda
5. feature
6. tracking
7. medications
8. application program
9. launch

B.
a. 〜を目玉とする；特徴づける
b. 計画する
c. 治療；療法
d. 応用プログラム
e. 軌道に乗せる；売り始める
f. 失敗
g. マスコミ報道
h. 課題；議題
i. 追跡調査する

Dialog: What Went Wrong?

Step 2　Dialog の中の空白に Key Expressions から当てはまる言葉を選びましょう。必要ならば語形を変えて入れてください。

Julie, Miguel, and Lara are in a meeting discussing their recent software launch.

Julie: So, the main item on our (A) (　　　　) today is to discuss how we can improve response to our latest (B) (　　　　) for dog owners.

Miguel: As you know, we haven't come anywhere close to our download target. When we (C) (　　　　) it in March, we (D) (　　　　) that, based on our market research, we would have 15,000 downloads by the end of June—at the very least. But the actual figure is less than half that. It's been a total (E) (　　　　).

Lara: If you ask me, we would have achieved much better results if we'd had more (F) (　　　　).

Julie: Exactly. We should have (G) (　　　　) the app in more magazines aimed at pet owners.

Miguel: You're both right. In addition, I'm sure it would have had more downloads if the functionality were better. Does anyone have any ideas?

Lara: I agree that the functions are a bit limited. So what if we were to include a health (H) (　　　　) function?

Julie: What use would that be?

Miguel: If owners had that, they could keep track of their dogs' weight, vaccination records, (I) (   ), and so on. That, I'm sure, would be really useful to the owners.

Julie: I see what you're saying. Great idea, Lara. Now we're getting somewhere!

Dialog Comprehension

Step 3　Dialogに関する次の質問に答えましょう。

1. What is the main topic of the conversation?
   (A) How to download a new app for pet owners
   (B) How to design a new product for pets
   (C) How to increase the number of downloads of a new app

2. What mistake do the speakers think they made?
   (A) They did not conduct sufficient market research.
   (B) They did not advertise widely enough.
   (C) They launched the app at the wrong time.

LISTENING SECTION

PART 1 Photographs（写真描写問題）（2問）

文を聞いて写真と一番一致するものを (A) (B) (C) (D) から選びなさい。

1. (A) (B) (C) (D)

2. (A) (B) (C) (D)

PART 2 Question-Response （応答問題）（3問）

質問または文を聞いて、一番適当と思われる応答を (A) (B) (C) から選びなさい。

1. (A) (B) (C)   2. (A) (B) (C)   3. (A) (B) (C)

PART 3 Conversation （会話問題）（3問）

会話文を聞いて質問に対する一番適当と思われる答えを (A) (B) (C) (D) から選びなさい。

Timetable: Horseferry to Walton Central

Departs	Arrives
09:00	10:23
09:40*	11:03
10:05	11:28
10:45*	12:08
11:20	12:35
12:05	13:28

*Mon.-Fri. only

1. Who most likely are the two speakers?
    (A) Colleagues in the same company
    (B) Friends from college
    (C) Rival company managers
    (D) A business owner and a lawyer

2. Where will the woman be next week?
    (A) In her office
    (B) In Germany
    (C) In China
    (D) On vacation

3. Look at the graphic. Which train bound for Walton Central is the woman most likely to take?
    (A) the 10:05
    (B) the 10:45
    (C) the 11:20
    (D) the 12:05

Unit 9

PART 4 Talks (説明文問題) (3問)

次のアナウンスメントを聞いて、質問に対する一番適当と思われる答を (A) (B) (C) (D) から選びなさい。

> ## METRO HEALTH CLUB & SPA
> ### Act now for our February Special!!
>
> Enrolment fee for new members – usually $120—now free!
>
> Monthly fees for the first six months – usually $80 per month—now just $50!
>
> And for current members, introduce a friend and get two free spa treatments worth up to $150!

1. Who is the speaker most likely addressing?
    - (A) Current health club members
    - (B) New health club members
    - (C) Health club junior staff
    - (D) Health club senior managers

2. Who was responsible for the mistake?
    - (A) The sales staff
    - (B) The reception staff
    - (C) The computer programmers
    - (D) The new members themselves

3. Look at the graphic. Compared with normal rates, how much is the first month's saving for new members?
    - (A) $120
    - (B) $150
    - (C) $180
    - (D) $200

READING SECTION

Grammar Points

TOEIC 頻出ポイント：Past Modals with "have"　過去完了形の文

could, would, may, might, must, should（助動詞）＋ have ＋過去分詞の形で、過去完了形の文に使われます。取っつきにくい文型で敬遠されがちですが、実はこの文型は、言い回しに気を使わなければならない、sophisticated な表現を必要とする、ビジネスシーンなどで一番日常的に使われる、とても会話的な表現なのです。次の5つのポイントを覚えましょう。

▶ Point 1　should (not) have+ 過去分詞の2つの文

〜すべきだった：	a. If you knew you were going to be late, you **should have called** me.
〜すべきでなかった：	b. You **shouldn't have eaten** that spicy food just before going to bed.
〜のはずだ：	c. The flight from New York **should have landed** by now.

▶ Point 2　must (not) have+ 過去分詞の文

〜であったに違いない：	d. Everyone's leaving the theater. The show **must have ended**.
〜でなかったに違いない：	e. Erik missed the party. He **must not have gotten** the invitation.

▶ Point 3　may/might (not) have+ 過去分詞の文

〜（だった）かもしれない：	f. I have to go back home. I think I **may/might have forgotten** to lock the door.
〜（ではなかった）のかもしれない：	g. The waiter hasn't taken my order yet. He **may/might not have seen** you.

▶ Point 4　would (not) have+ 過去分詞：仮定法過去完了の文

〜することになっただろうに：	h. If the driver hadn't reacted so quickly, he **would have hit** the other car.
〜しなかっただろうに：	i. If the road hadn't been so icy, I **wouldn't have slipped and fallen off** my bicycle.

▶ Point 5　could have+ 過去分詞：仮定法過去完了の文

〜できただろうに：	j. The robber **could have escaped** if he had run faster.

Grammar Quiz (5問)

次の文を読んで、一番適当と思われる語を選びなさい。

1. I feel a little feverish. I think I ------- have caught a cold.
   (A) would
   (B) may
   (C) should
   (D) will

2. If Harry hadn't taken a flashlight with him, he ------- have gotten lost on the dark trail.
   (A) shall
   (B) must
   (C) will
   (D) would

3. A virus just infected my computer. I ------- have clicked on that suspicious link.
   (A) might not
   (B) would not
   (C) should not
   (D) could not

4. Gerry isn't answering my calls. He ------- have put his cellphone on silent mode.
   (A) should
   (B) would
   (C) must
   (D) can

5. If Bob had known the movie was so scary, he ------- not have gone to see it.
   (A) could
   (B) would
   (C) should
   (D) must

PART 5 Incomplete Sentences (短文穴埋め問題) (2問)

次の文の空欄に一番適当と思われる答を (A) (B) (C) (D) から選びなさい。

1. I ------- have bought a more powerful computer, because this one is too slow.
   (A) should
   (B) would
   (C) could
   (D) may

2. If I had known you didn't drink coffee, I would have ------- some tea for you.
   (A) make
   (B) made
   (C) to make
   (D) making

PART 6 Text Completion (長文穴埋め問題) (4問)

次の文の4つの空欄に一番適当と思われる答を (A) (B) (C) (D) から選びなさい。

Text: Article

"I ---1.--- have stayed longer!" This must be the final thought of every visitor as they are leaving the beautiful town of Zermatt in the Swiss Alps. Surrounded by snow-capped mountains, huge glaciers, and lush green meadows, Zermatt is one of the ---2.--- spectacular tourist destinations in the world. It offers a whole range of outdoor activities such as skiing, hiking, climbing, and hang gliding. But if you're not in the mood or the type for such active pursuits, you can relax on the terrace of your hotel or ---3.--- Swiss cuisine in one of Zermatt's many great restaurants. ---4.--- You must leave your car in a parking lot and then take a special mountain train to get there.

1. (A) must
   (B) might
   (C) would
   (D) should

2. (A) most
   (B) much
   (C) more
   (D) many

3. (A) enjoy
   (B) enjoys
   (C) enjoyed
   (D) enjoying

4. (A) Switzerland is not really very well known for its cuisine.
   (B) The restaurants all offer free valet parking.
   (C) Another bonus is that the town is entirely car-free.
   (D) The only way to reach the city is by car.

Unit 9

PART 7 Reading Comprehension（読解問題）（5問）

次の３つの文書を読んで、一番適当と思われる答を (A) (B) (C) (D) から選びなさい。

Material 1:

E-mail 1
To: Anna Bautista
From: Felix Nussbaum
Subject: Conference schedule
Dear Ms. Bautista: I am contacting you in connection with my presentation at the upcoming conference on Wednesday, June 12. As you know, I'm scheduled to give the first presentation at 10:00 A.M. on opening day. I was planning to fly from Kansas City to Denver the evening before the conference, but unfortunately, that will no longer be possible, as I have been asked to attend a government-sponsored meeting of climate scientists in Washington, D.C. that day. However, I have found a flight from Washington that gets me into Denver at around 11:30 A.M. on the day of the conference. I was therefore wondering if it might be possible for you to reschedule my presentation for some time in the afternoon. I am truly sorry for letting you know at such short notice, but the invitation to attend the Washington meeting was one that would have been impossible for me to refuse. Kind regards, Dr. Felix Nussbaum

Material 2: Document

Colorado Climate Change Symposium
Plenary Program
Wednesday, June 12, 2017

Time	Speaker	Topic
10:00-11:00	Dr. Felix Nussbaum	New developments in carbon capture
11:15-12:15	Dr. Emily Cho	Glacial melting in Greenland: Some countermeasures
1:30-2:30	Dr. Eric Mulvaney	Consequences of Himalayan deforestation
2:45-3:45	Dr. Elizabeth Yates	Canada's resource conservation program
4:15-5:15	Dr. Michel Tavernier	New climate initiatives from the EU
5:30-6:30	Dr. Deepak Chaudhury	India's growing solar industry

Material 3:

E-mail 2
From: Eric Mulvaney
To: Anna Bautista
Subject: Change of schedule
Dear Ms. Bautista: Thank you for your message regarding a change in schedule for the opening day of the conference. I realize how difficult it must be for you to deal with such last-minute schedule changes. Although I quite understand Dr. Nussbaum's reasons, and as much as I would like to comply with your request, I am afraid I am unable to switch from the afternoon to the 10:00 slot because my flight gets in at 9:00 A.M. that morning, and there is no way I would be able to reach the venue in time. But I think I have a solution. Dr. Emily Cho, the second speaker, is a good friend of mine, and I know that she plans to arrive in Denver on the previous day. I took the liberty of approaching her privately to ask if she would be prepared to take the opening slot, and she agreed. Therefore, if it is acceptable to you, Dr. Cho and I will take the first and second slots, respectively, enabling Dr. Nussbaum to take my current slot in the afternoon. Kind regards, Dr. Eric Mulvaney

1. What will likely be the new order of speakers at the conference?
   (A) Nussbaum, Cho, Mulvaney, Yates
   (B) Mulvaney, Cho, Yates, Nussbaum
   (C) Cho, Mulvaney, Nussbaum, Yates
   (D) Cho, Mulvaney, Yates, Nussbaum

2. What is Dr. Nussbaum's reason for requesting the schedule change?
   (A) He has a personal matter to deal with.
   (B) He has had to change his travel plans.
   (C) Another speaker wants to take his slot.
   (D) The flight he booked has been cancelled.

3. How does Dr. Mulvaney offer to solve the problem with the 10:00 A.M. slot?
   (A) Take it himself
   (B) Find a new speaker
   (C) Ask another speaker to take it
   (D) Ask Dr. Nussbaum to reconsider

4. Where will Dr. Nussbaum be on the day before the conference?
   (A) Kansas City
   (B) Denver
   (C) Washington, D.C.
   (D) It is not mentioned.

5. Which word or phrase is closest in meaning to "as much as" as it is used in passage 3, line 5?
   (A) even though
   (B) apparently
   (C) consequently
   (D) due to the fact that

TOEIC のための満点アプリ
PART 7 Reading Comprehension 読解問題

▶設問は次の 4 種類に分かれます
1. 要約を求める大きな問題
2. 詳細な情報を求める小さな問題
3. NOT を含む質問
4. 語彙の意味を問う質問

▶要約を求める大きい問題
質問はパッセージに書かれてある順番に並んでいます。まず始めの要約に関する質問の答えは第 1 パラグラフ中にあると考えましょう。またそれはそのパッセージの主旨でもある大きな問題です。
* 例外として、第 1 問が宛名、差出人、用件に関するものであることもあります。

▶詳細な情報を求める小さい問題
英語でパラグラフを新しくするというこは、場面が展開するということです。そして小さい質問は各パラグラフごとに設定されていることが多いのです。質問を読んで、その答えになるキーワードを各パラグラフから見つけましょう。慣れれば難解な質問は数問にすぎず、パッセージ中の語彙をそのまま、または、パラフレーズ（言い換え）したものが正解として選択肢に入っているのが拾えるようになるでしょう。

Unit 10
Innovations and Technology

Key Expressions

Step 1　A 欄の語彙に合う訳を B 欄から選びましょう。

A.
1. user-friendly
2. constantly
3. keen on
4. appeal (to someone)
5. selection
6. hang on
7. copyright
8. extensive
9. classic

B.
a. 惹きつける；好まれる
b. 利用しやすい；使いやすい
c. ずっと持ち続ける；持ちこたえる
d. 広範囲の；多方面の
e. 古典の
f. 撰集：集めたもの
g. 興味を持っている
h. 著作権
i. 絶えず；常に

Dialog: Watching Movies on DVD or on Streaming Services

Step 2　Dialog の中の空白に Key Expressions から当てはまる言葉を選びましょう。必要ならば語形を変えて入れてください。

Two colleagues, Russell and Elena, are chatting at the office.

Russell: Did you do anything exciting over the weekend, Elena?

Elena: Well, I'm a real movie fan, as you know, so I spent Sunday evening watching movies. I have a really (A) (　　　　) collection of DVDs.

Russell: You still watch DVDs? I thought people had stopped doing that. Everyone I know is using video streaming services*. They have a great (B) (　　　　), and they're also really convenient – you just pay a monthly subscription fee and watch as many movies and TV shows as you like. And at any time you like.

Elena: Yes, I know. I've tried most of them.

Russell: So, I guess you didn't like them. Why are you still (C) (　　　　) to your DVDs?

Elena: Well, I know that the subscription services are convenient and (D) (　　　　), and I'd probably spend more time watching them—if, that is, they had more content that I like.

Russell: But they're (E) (　　　　) adding new shows and movies. Surely you can find something that (F) (　　　　) to you.

Elena: The thing is, I'm mainly interested in (G) (　　　　) movies, particularly from the 60s and 70s. If you look at the movies that the streaming services offer, it's hard to find many films that were made before the 1980s.

Russell: Well, now that you mention it, I suppose you're right.

Elena: Maybe I'm an exception—I'm sure that most of the streaming-service customers are (H) (　　　) modern content.

Russell: Why do you think there are so few older movies?

Elena: I'm not an expert, but I heard that it's complicated and expensive to get permission to stream older movies because of (I) (　　　) laws.

Russell: Well, for your sake then, let's hope they don't stop making DVD players—or DVDs!

*video streaming service ビデオ配信サービス；映像配信

Dialog Comprehension

Step 3　Dialog に関する次の質問に答えましょう。

1. Why is Russell surprised?
   (A) Elena knows so much about copyright law.
   (B) Elena is still using what he thinks is old-fashioned technology.
   (C) Elena has never even heard of video streaming technology.

2. What can be reasonably inferred about Elena?
   (A) She has never watched a movie on a streaming service.
   (B) She thinks streaming services are much too expensive
   (C) She is not a big fan of movies made aftre1980.

LISTENING SECTION

PART 1 Photographs （写真描写問題）（2問）

文を聞いて写真と一番一致するものを (A) (B) (C) (D) から選びなさい。

1. (A) (B) (C) (D)

2. (A) (B) (C) (D)

PART 2 Question-Response （応答問題）（3問）

質問または文を聞いて、一番適当と思われる応答を (A) (B) (C) から選びなさい。

1. (A) (B) (C)   2. (A) (B) (C)   3. (A) (B) (C)

PART 3 Conversation （会話問題）（3問）

会話文を聞いて質問に対する一番適当と思われる答えを (A) (B) (C) (D) から選びなさい。

Running Starts: Sunday, June 17

Distance	5.84 miles	Duration	58:52
Average speed	9.9 miles per hour	Calories burned	647 kcal

1. What physical activities does Emilio like to do?
   (A) Running and swimming
   (B) Swimming and weight training
   (C) Cycling and swimming
   (D) Weight training and cycling

2. What does Emilio express an interest in doing?
   (A) Taking up swimming
   (B) Training with Gwen
   (C) Using fitness technology
   (D) Exercising even harder

3. Look at the graphic. What information about her run did Gwen NOT give Emilio?
   (A) How far she ran
   (B) For how long she ran
   (C) Her running pace
   (D) How much energy she used

Unit 10

PART 4 Talks （説明文問題）（3問）

 65

次のアナウンスメントを聞いて、質問に対する一番適当と思われる答を (A) (B) (C) (D) から選びなさい。

1. Where would listeners be most likely to hear this talk?
    (A) On the radio
    (B) On television
    (C) In a theater
    (D) On a computer

2. What is one advantage of the product that is being described?
    (A) It will show users how to distinguish between good and bad apps.
    (B) It offers apps at a lower price than the original app maker.
    (C) It will give users easy access to 30 useful apps.
    (D) It will make apps run more quickly and efficiently.

3. How much will it cost users to start using the new product?
    (A) Nothing
    (B) $10
    (C) $30
    (D) $50

TOEIC のための満点アプリ

一つの語彙でも違う意味を持つものに注意しましょう

TOEIC テストを始め英語力テストは語彙の勝負であるとも言えます。
TOEIC テストで避けては通れないのが、paraphrase（言い換え）です、例えば PART 2 の設問での例。選択肢には mean の 3 つの意味が使われていて受験者を迷わせます。

　I don't quite understand what you <u>mean</u>.（おっしゃった<u>意味</u>がよく分かりません。）
　　(A) Tell me what the <u>mean</u> score is.（<u>標準値</u>を教えて下さい。）
　　(B) "Enormous" <u>means</u> "very big."（"Enormous" は "とても大きい" という<u>意味</u>です。）
　　(C) I didn't want to be <u>mean</u>.（<u>意地悪</u>をするつもりではなかったのですが。）
　正解は (B)

以下の単語は、基礎レベルのものばかりですが、TOEIC テストでは様々な意味で使われます。辞書でしっかり確認しておきましょう。

mean	意味する・標準値・意地悪な	fine	細かい・立派な・罰金
call	呼ぶ・電話する・鳥の鳴き声	labor	労働・陣痛・努力する
change	変わる・小銭・おつり	mind	心・気にかける・〜の世話をする
bill	請求書・議案・紙幣	order	注文・順序・整頓 /（生物学）目
bite	噛む・軽い食事・分け前	rest	休む・残り・（音楽の）休止符
fair	展示会・美人の・まあまあの	save	救う・倹約する・〜を除いて
file	書類綴じ・提訴する・やすり	work	働く・（機械が）きちんと動く・作品

READING SECTION

Grammar Points

TOEIC 頻出のポイント：Conditional Sentences　条件文（仮定法）

実社会に出てみると、条件文というのは、日常の会話で絶対に避けて通れないものなのです。相手に何かお願いしたり、提案したりするときに丁寧な言い方として、一番必要なのは、この条件文、とくに第2条件文（過去仮定法）なのです。
Could you come in at 10 tomorrow morning?（明日朝10時にお越し頂けますか。）
などというのはその一例です。またていねいな表現以外にもビジネス関係で確約を与えたくない時などは、第2条件文を巧く使います。It would be nice if we could do business with you.（ご一緒にお仕事が出来ると宜しいですね。）その本音は「あまりそういうチャンスはないかもしれない」または、「ビジネスをしたくない。」です。もっと前向きな気持ちがあれば、It will be so nice to do business with you. というべきでしょう。

このユニットでは会話で大切な第2条件文、また少し高度な第3条件文について学習しましょう。

▶ Point 1-1　現実的でない条件（第2条件文）Imaginary or Unreal Conditions

これらの文では想像上の仮定の条件について話します。
If + 主語 + 動詞の過去形，主語 + **would** + 動詞の原形

a. **If** our CEO **left** the company, it **would be** hard to replace him.（想像）

b. **If** we **upgraded** our computer system, our productivity **would increase**.（仮定）

▶ Point 1-2　were to+ 動詞の原形を使った第2条件文

Point 1-1 a. b. の文は were to を使って次のように書き換えることも出来ます。

a'. If our CEO **were to leave** the company, I'm sure our stock price would fall.

b'. If we **were to upgrade** our computer system, our productivity would increase.

▶ Point 1-3　第2条件文では was も were になる

第2条件文では I, you, she, he, it, they などに付く be 動詞は全て **were** になります。

c. If I **were** you, I would not eat too much salty food. It will raise your blood pressure.

▶ Point 2　もう変えることの出来ない過去完了の文（第3条件文）Impossible Conditions

「あの時〜していたらこうはならなかっただろう」「あの時〜しなかったらこうなっていただろう」と全て過去に起こったこと、変えられない過去の事実について話している。
If + 主語 +*had done*（動詞の過去完了形），主語 + *would*（助動詞）+ *have done*（完了形）

d. **If** you **had checked** your phone, you **would have seen** my message.

e. **If** I **had not remembered** to send in the application form, I **would not have been** able to take the test.

▶ Point 3　if を省略した条件文も、ビジネスレターなどに使われます

この場合主語と動詞（または助動詞）の位置が反対になるので注意しましょう

f. **Were you** to reconsider my offer to buy your apartment, I would be very pleased to hear from you.

g. **Had I** received your invitation earlier, I would have been delighted to attend the party.

Unit 10

Grammar Quiz (5問)

次の文を読んで、一番適当と思われる語を選びなさい。

1. I wouldn't travel to that part of the world right now if I ------- you. I hear it's not safe.
   (A) am
   (B) was
   (C) were
   (D) would be

2. ------- jumped out of the way in time, that car would have hit me.
   (A) Had I not
   (B) Were I not
   (C) If had I not
   (D) If I were not

3. If you ------- lose your job tomorrow, what would you do?
   (A) had
   (B) will
   (C) are to
   (D) were to

4. If Sam ------- more supporting evidence, he could have gotten a much higher grade on his essay.
   (A) includes
   (B) had included
   (C) has included
   (D) were included

5. If I had not taken your excellent advice, I ------- a published author.
   (A) never became
   (B) will never become
   (C) would never become
   (D) would never have become

PART 5 Incomplete Sentences (短文穴埋め問題) (2問)

次の文の空欄に一番適当と思われる答を (A) (B) (C) (D) から選びなさい。

1. Some people worry that: If machines ------- to become too intelligent, they might take over the world.
   (A) are
   (B) were
   (C) would
   (D) will

2. I can't wait for the day ------- all cars become driverless.
   (A) when
   (B) which
   (C) that
   (D) where

PART 6 Text Completion (長文穴埋め問題) (4問)

次の文の4つの空欄に一番適当と思われる答を (A) (B) (C) (D) から選びなさい。

Text: Letter

Hi Meg,

Thanks for emailing me and asking how I am after my cycling accident. -------1.-, I didn't break any bones or suffer any other serious injuries. I just have a few cuts and bruises. It happened when my bike skidded on a wet, slippery road -------2.- I was riding down a hill on my way home from school. Naturally, if I had known it was going to rain that evening, I would have left my bike at home and taken the bus. -------3.- Thankfully, I was wearing my helmet (as I always do, of course!), and there were no other vehicles near me when I fell into the road. I'll soon be -------4.- again, but I'll make sure to check the weather forecast first!

Best,

Abdul

1. (A) By the way
   (B) All the same
   (C) Fortunately
   (D) However

2. (A) since
   (B) during
   (C) after
   (D) as

3. (A) Buses in this town aren't very convenient.
   (B) My bike wasn't damaged too badly.
   (C) It was the second time I have had an accident while riding my bike.
   (D) Still, it could have been a lot worse.

4. (A) ride
   (B) rides
   (C) ridden
   (D) riding

PART 7 Reading Comprehension（読解問題）（5問）

次の3つの文書を読んで、一番適当と思われる答を (A) (B) (C) (D) から選びなさい。

Material1:

E-mail 1
To: Kelly Harper
From: Lizzie Gandolfo
Subject: Advice, please!
Hi Kelly, How are things? I hope you and your family are well. I'm writing to ask your advice. Not too long ago, Robert and I came into a small sum of money from an inheritance, so now we have a few thousand dollars that we would like to spend on home improvements. I've heard a lot recently about smart homes, and they seem like a really convenient and exciting idea. The only problem is that neither Robert nor I am very tech-savvy, so we're hesitant to move ahead with having smart devices installed before we know a bit more about the advantages and disadvantages of doing it. I remember your telling me last year that you had decided to upgrade your home with various smart devices, and so I was wondering how you were finding it. Could you give me some idea of the good and bad points so that Robert and I can decide if it will be a good investment for us or not? Looking forward to hearing from you. Best, Lizzie

Material 2:

E-mail 2
To: Lizzie Gandolfo
From: Kelly Harper
Subect: Re: Advice, please!

Hi Lizzie,

Nice to hear from you! It's been a while. Here, for what it's worth, is what I've discovered through my experience with smart-home technology. There are certainly a lot of advantages. When you convert your home into a smart home, you can program all your devices to fit your needs, which means that you can control your home wherever you happen to be. One great advantage is that having the ability to put devices like thermostats, air conditioners, and lighting on a timer means that you can turn them on and off when you're away from home, which can save you money on your electricity bills. Also, almost all smart-home products are easy to install. You probably won't even need a specialist.

But there are also disadvantages. It will definitely cost you quite a bit to buy a complete smart-home system. In addition, though most systems are not complicated to use, if neither of you is tech-savvy (as you say), you'll probably have to spend a lot of time reading manuals or calling a helpline. All in all, I think smart homes are great, but they aren't for everyone.

However, if you'd really like to try, I'd suggest that you start in a small way by getting a "smart" home-security system that will provide cameras and sensors to protect your home. These systems are reasonably priced and easy to monitor. Once you get comfortable with this system, you can start adding extra devices. Anyway, check out the attached link, which has some information about the various systems that are available.

Best,

Kelly

Material 3: Chart

	SafeHome	KeySure	Sekurit	Home Watch
Equipment costs	$550	$350	$260	$230
Monthly costs	$35	$30	$28	$30
Professional Installation included in price	X	O	O	X
Environmental Sensors	O	O	O	O
Power Outage Backup	O	O	O	X

1. Why has Lizzie recently become interested in carrying out some home improvements?
   (A) She and Robert just got married.
   (B) She and Robert have bought a new house.
   (C) She received some money unexpectedly.
   (D) She envies her friend's smart-home system.

2. Which of these does Kelly NOT mention as an advantage of having a smart home?
   (A) Power bills may become cheaper.
   (B) Smart devices can be controlled remotely.
   (C) Equipping a house with a smart system is relatively inexpensive.
   (D) Some devices can be installed without professional assistance.

3. Why does Kelly think a smart-house system may cause problems for Lizzie and Robert?
   (A) They may not have enough money to install one.
   (B) Their house is not suitable for installing such a system.
   (C) She has had some problems with her own system.
   (D) Kelly and Robert may lack the necessary technical skills and knowledge.

4. Which of the following words is closest in meaning to "hesitant" as it is used in passage 1, line 7?
   (A) keen
   (B) reluctant
   (C) ignorant
   (D) unaware

5. Look at the chart. If Lizzie wants a lower-priced system without set-up costs, which company will she most likely choose?
   (A) SafeHome
   (B) KeySure
   (C) Sekurit
   (D) Home Watch

Review Test 2 (Units 6-10)

LISTENING SECTION (20 questions)

PART 1 Photographs （写真描写問題）（2問）

文を聞いて次の写真と一番一致する文を選びなさい。

1. (A) (B) (C) (D)

2. (A) (B) (C) (D)

PART 2 Question-Response （応答問題）（6問）

質問または文を聞いて、一番適当と思われる応答を (A) (B) (C) から選びなさい。

3. (A) (B) (C)   4. (A) (B) (C)   5. (A) (B) (C)
6. (A) (B) (C)   7. (A) (B) (C)   8. (A) (B) (C)

PART 3 Conversations （会話問題）（2Converssation × 3問＝6問）

表を見ながら会話文を聞いて質問に対する一番適当と思われる答を (A) (B) (C) (D) から選びなさい。

Conversation 1:

Adkins Diet	Caveman Diet	Vegan Diet	Weight Winners Diet
A lot of meat and fish	Meat, fish only	No meat, fish	Some meat, fish
Some vegetables	No vegetables	A lot of vegetables	Some vegetables
No fruit	No fruit	A lot of fruit	Some fruit
A little starch	No starch	Some starch	Some starch
No dairy products	No dairy products	No dairy products	Some dairy products

9. Which diet does the man prefer?
   (A) The Vegan
   (B) The Adkins
   (C) The Caveman
   (D) The Weight Winners

10. Look at the chart. Which two diets might be considered opposites?
    (A) Caveman and Adkins
    (B) Weight Winners and Vegan
    (C) Caveman and Vegan
    (D) Adkins and Weight Winners

11. What do all the diets have in common?
    (A) No dairy foods
    (B) No fried foods
    (C) Large amounts of protein
    (D) A large variety of foods to choose from

表を見ながら会話文を聞いて質問に対する一番適当と思われる答を (A) (B) (C) (D) から選びなさい。

Conversation 2:

A. 2 movies / month	$7
B. 5 movies / month	$20
C. 10 movies / month	$25

12. What are the speakers trying to decide?
    (A) Which movie to watch this weekend
    (B) Which movie streaming service to buy
    (C) How many DVDs to check out from the library
    (D) What to do next weekend

13. How many movies does the man want to watch?
    (A) One movie a month
    (B) Ten movies a month
    (C) Five movies a week
    (D) One movie a week

14. Look at the chart. Which option will they most likely choose?
    - (A) A
    - (B) B
    - (C) C
    - (D) None of them

PART 4 Talks （説明文問題）（3問）（2 Talks × 3問＝ 6問）

次のアナウンスメントを聞いて、質問に対する一番適当と思われる答を (A) (B) (C) (D) から選びなさい。

Announcement 1:

15. Where is this announcement being made?
    - (A) In a company head office
    - (B) On a radio program
    - (C) On a university campus
    - (D) In a shopping mall

16. Who should apply for this internship?
    - (A) Citizens of San Diego
    - (B) Solar engineers
    - (C) College students
    - (D) Computer scientists

17. Which of these kinds of work does the announcement say that the interns will do?
    - (A) Conduct surveys
    - (B) Install solar panels
    - (C) Take orders for solar-panel sales
    - (D) Organize computer skills courses

次のアナウンスメントを聞いて、質問に対する一番適当と思われる答を (A) (B) (C) (D) から選びなさい。

Announcement 2:

18. How many special Valentine's deals are mentioned?
    - (A) 1
    - (B) 2
    - (C) 3
    - (D) 4

19. Who is this announcement primarily intended for?
    (A) Women shopping for gifts for men
    (B) Men shopping for gifts for women
    (C) Parents shopping for gifts for children
    (D) Children shopping for gifts for parents

20. How much does the 2-ounce box cost?
    (A) $3.95
    (B) $4.00
    (C) $6.00
    (D) $12.95

READING SECTION (20 questions)

PART 5 Incomplete Sentences (短文穴埋め問題)（2 問）

次の文の空欄に一番適当と思われる言葉を (A) (B) (C) (D) から選んで入れなさい。

21. Be careful when opening the overhead bins, as the contents ------- during the flight and could fall out and cause injury.
    (A) are shifting
    (B) may have shifted
    (C) had shifted
    (D) will be shifted

22. One of ------- in today's *Times* ------- about the negative effects of light pollution on migrating birds.
    (A) the article … was
    (B) article … was
    (C) the articles … were
    (D) the articles … was

PART 6 Text Completion (長文穴埋め問題)（2 Text × 4 問＝ 8 問）

次の文の空欄に一番適当と思われる答を (A) (B) (C) (D) から選びなさい。

Selection 1:
Text: Advertisement

Do you often travel abroad on business? Do you worry because you don't speak the language of the country you are in? ------- (23.) there is an app just for you. It's called the Translapp. For only $55.95 a month, you can subscribe to this superb translation service. Then, when you return home from your trip, if you no longer need the service, simply ------- (24.) the subscription. Here is how it works. Pick two languages: the language you speak and the language you want to translate into. You can choose either voice or text translation. ------- (25.) You will then hear a live person instantly translate your words. To have another person's words translated, simply hold up your phone and have the person ------- (26.) into the microphone. In seconds, you will hear the other person's words translated into your language.

23. (A) That's because
    (B) Now
    (C) Otherwise,
    (D) Recently,

24. (A) subscribe to
    (B) add
    (C) pay for
    (D) cancel

25. (A) For voice, you just speak the information you want to communicate into the microphone.
    (B) For text, translate what you want to say into the desired language on your own.
    (C) Some languages may not be available for translation.
    (D) Select all of the countries that you are planning to travel to.

26. (A) speaking
    (B) speak
    (C) to speak
    (D) speaks

Selection 2:
Text: Article

I don't usually write product reviews, but in this case, I have to make an exception. The KitchenMaster Pro Chef's Knife is quite simply the best knife I have ------- used. I am not a professional, but cooking is a serious hobby for me. I've owned many knives over the past 30 years, but not one of them has been nearly as good as this one. The regular price is $550, but I bought mine when it was ------- special offer for just $225. But let me just say that if I had known beforehand what an outstanding knife this is, I ------- still have been willing to pay the full price for it. ------- Whether you're a professional or an amateur in the kitchen, this knife is a cook's dream come true.

27. (A) always   28. (A) on   29. (A) should
    (B) even   (B) at   (B) would
    (C) just   (C) in   (C) must
    (D) ever   (D) by   (D) could

30. (A) If you're looking for the best knife money can buy, don't hesitate to get your Pro Chef's Knife today.
    (B) This knife would not suit everyone's kitchen and cooking needs, however.
    (C) I've never bought such an expensive knife before.
    (D) Unfortunately, this knife is no longer available to non-professionals.

PART 7 Reading Comprehension 読解問題（10問）

次の３つの文書を読んで、一番適当と思われる答を (A) (B) (C) (D) から選びなさい。

Selection 1:
Material 1: Notice

> Prairie Steakhouse now hiring for our Oakville location!
> Position: Restaurant Manager
> Outstanding benefits!
>   Competitive Pay
>   Paid vacation, sick leave, and family leave
>   Medical / Dental coverage
> Minimum 4 years' restaurant experience
> At least 1 year in restaurant management
> Knowledge of food safety and federal food-safety regulations
> High-school diploma
> Apply online: http://www.PrairieSteakhr@mail.com/
>   or send email to hr@PrairieSteak.com.

Material 2:

E-mail
To: hr@PrairieSteak.com
From: Jen Page
Subject: Re: Manager's position
Date: March 5

To Whom It May Concern:

I am responding to your job notice for the position of manager of the Prairie Steakhouse as published in the March 4 edition of the *Oakville Town News*. I have lived in Oakville all my life, and I have eaten many fine meals at Prairie Steakhouse. It has long been my dream to work as a manager at your esteemed restaurant. I have had extensive experience in restaurant work, beginning as a waitperson at Bob's Diner when I was a high-school student. I graduated from Oakville Community College with an Associates Degree in Restaurant Management. While working toward my degree, I had a work-study assignment as head server at the College Café, followed by an internship as an assistant manager at Hamburger Happiness. Since graduating, I have been the assistant manager at Family Pizza. I work well with people, and I have an excellent eye for the many tasks that a manager needs to carry out in a fast-paced environment such as a larger, popular restaurant like the Prairie Steakhouse. My resume is attached. Kindly consider my application.

Sincerely,
Jen Page

Review Test 2 (Units 6-10)

Material 3: Resume

> **Resume of Jen Page for position of Manager at Prairie Steakhouse**
> Email: Jen45Page@mail.com
> Phone: 555-5522
>
> Education
>   Oakville Community College, Associates Degree 2015
>   Oakville High School, graduated 2013
>
> Work Experience
>   Assistant Manager, Family Pizza, September 2015- present
>   Assistant Manager, Hamburger Happiness, January 2015-June 2015
>   Head Server, College Café, 2014
>   Waitperson, Bob's Diner, 2011 – 2013
>
> References:
>   1. Craig Baker, Family Pizza 555-5255
>   2. Lynn Hutton, Hamburger Happiness 555-2252
>   3. Kathy Claymore, College Café 555-2525

31. Which of these job qualifications is Not mentioned in Jen's letter and resume?
    (A) Experience as a waitperson
    (B) Experience in restaurant management
    (C) Knowledge of food safety
    (D) Education background

32. According to the job notice, what benefit is NOT offered?
    (A) Dental coverage
    (B) Pension
    (C) Health insurance
    (D) Leave of absence

33. Which word is closest in meaning to "competitive" as used in Line 4 of the job notice?
    (A) aggressive
    (B) rival
    (C) equal
    (D) reasonable

34. How long did Jen serve as an intern?
    (A) Three months
    (B) Six months
    (C) One year
    (D) Three years

35. Based on her email and resume, which statement is true about Jen?
    (A) She likes the food at Prairie Steakhouse.
    (B) She has heard of the Prairie Steakhouse but has never eaten there.
    (C) While in college, she was a server at Prairie Steakhouse.
    (D) She once had a dream that she was a waitperson at Prairie Steakhouse.

次の３つの文書を読んで、一番適当と思われる答を (A) (B) (C) (D) から選びなさい。

Selection 2:
Material 1: Announcement

> The Southwestern States Green Energy Expo is being held at the Sandy Gulch Convention Center in Phoenix, March 2-4. This event showcases products offered by renewable-energy, clean-power, and energy-conservation industries, among others. Exhibitors will include manufacturers and dealers of related products and services such as transportation, solar and wind technologies, and building efficiency. Last year's expo saw a record 11,000 visitors. Organized by CleanPlanetCo-op. Send requests for booth bookings to expo@CleanPlanet.org.

Material 2:

E-mail 1
To: Cary Maples, Ted Brown
From: Jean Aldwich
Subject: Green Energy Expo booth

Dear Cary and Ted,
Our booth is going to be Number 21, in the northwest corner of the room, near the restrooms. It's smaller than last year's, so we'll need only you two there. I've already informed Melinda that she won't be needed this year. Also, with such a small booth in an out-of-the-way location like this, it is tempting for us to wander off and try to hand out brochures on the exposition floor. This is very bad manners at an expo, as it gets in the way of exhibitors that have paid more for their booth. So I'm just reminding you to stay at our booth. While the above may sound discouraging, the positive side of our location is that others will be less likely to be blocking our booth. Good luck, and keep smiling.

All the best,
Jean

Material 3:

E-mail 2
To: Jean Aldwich
From: Susan Henderson
Subject: Re: Booth at Green Energy Expo
Hi, Jean, Cary shared your e-mail regarding the booth we've been assigned at Green Energy Expo. I'm afraid I'm going to have to step in here. Instead of subjecting our staff to unsatisfactory working conditions and putting our company at a disadvantage, I would rather pay more and get a booth in a more advantageous location. I have cleared the funds with the budget director and secured a far better booth. You have been reassigned to Booth 5, to the immediate right of the main entrance, where everyone will see it. (See the attached confirmation and map.) Booth 5 has almost twice as much space as the one previously booked. Please send out an email ASAP to Cary, Ted, and Melinda, informing them of this change. In particular, be sure that Melinda knows she will be working at the booth. And apologize for the inconvenience. I need to be cc'd in on this email and all future emails pertaining to the Green Energy Expo set up. Susan Henderson, Manager Marketing

36. Who is the announcement attended for?
    (A) Visitors to Sandy Gulch Convention Center
    (B) Environmental studies majors
    (C) Consumers of green-technology products and devices
    (D) Companies that want to exhibit at the expo

37. What does Jean say about Booth Number 21?
    (A) It will be blocked by people waiting to get into the restrooms.
    (B) It was the only booth still available.
    (C) It is small and out of the way.
    (D) It will attract visitors with bad manners.

38. How does Jean expect Cary and Ted to react to her email?
    (A) They will be glad not to have to work with Melinda.
    (B) They will be pleased with the less-busy location.
    (C) They will not care one way or the other.
    (D) They may be a little disappointed.

39. What attitude does Susan express in her email?
    (A) Disapproval
    (B) Approval
    (C) Uncertainty
    (D) Friendliness

40. In what way is Booth 5 better than Booth 21?
    (A) It is in the center of the expo floor.
    (B) It is closer to the restrooms.
    (C) It offers better working conditions in every way.
    (D) It is lower-priced and has more brochures.

Review Test 1 (Unit 1〜5)

LISTENING SECTION

Part 1
No.	ANSWER
1	A B C D
2	A B C D

Part 2
No.	ANSWER
3	A B C
4	A B C
5	A B C
6	A B C
7	A B C
8	A B C

Part 3
No.	ANSWER
9	A B C D
10	A B C D
11	A B C D
12	A B C D
13	A B C D
14	A B C D

Part 4
No.	ANSWER
15	A B C D
16	A B C D
17	A B C D
18	A B C D
19	A B C D
20	A B C D

READING SECTION

Part 5
No.	ANSWER
21	A B C D
22	A B C D

Part 6
No.	ANSWER
23	A B C D
24	A B C D
25	A B C D
26	A B C D
27	A B C D
28	A B C D
29	A B C D
30	A B C D

Part 7
No.	ANSWER
31	A B C D
32	A B C D
33	A B C D
34	A B C D
35	A B C D
36	A B C D
37	A B C D
38	A B C D
39	A B C D
40	A B C D

正解数　　／40問

Review Test 2 (Unit 6〜10)

LISTENING SECTION

Part 1
No.	ANSWER
1	A B C D
2	A B C D

Part 2
No.	ANSWER
3	A B C
4	A B C
5	A B C
6	A B C
7	A B C
8	A B C

Part 3
No.	ANSWER
9	A B C D
10	A B C D
11	A B C D
12	A B C D
13	A B C D
14	A B C D

Part 4
No.	ANSWER
15	A B C D
16	A B C D
17	A B C D
18	A B C D
19	A B C D
20	A B C D

READING SECTION

Part 5
No.	ANSWER
21	A B C D
22	A B C D

Part 6
No.	ANSWER
23	A B C D
24	A B C D
25	A B C D
26	A B C D
27	A B C D
28	A B C D
29	A B C D
30	A B C D

Part 7
No.	ANSWER
31	A B C D
32	A B C D
33	A B C D
34	A B C D
35	A B C D
36	A B C D
37	A B C D
38	A B C D
39	A B C D
40	A B C D

正解数　　／40問

著作権法上、無断複写・複製は禁じられています。

\multicolumn{3}{l}{TOEIC® L&R Test: On Target \<Book 2\> [Revised Edition]}	[B-874]
\multicolumn{4}{l}{TOEIC® テスト：オン・ターゲット \<Book 2\>［改訂版］}
1　刷	\multicolumn{3}{l}{2019年 4月 1日}
7　刷	\multicolumn{3}{l}{2024年 3月 29日}
著　者	大賀　リヱ		Rie Ooga
	ウィリアム J. ベンフィールド		William J. Benfield
	アン N. グリースン		Ann N. Gleason
	テリー L. ブラウニング		Terry L. Browning
	デイビット　セイン		David Thayne
発行者	\multicolumn{3}{l}{南雲　一範　　Kazunori Nagumo}
発行所	\multicolumn{3}{l}{株式会社　南雲堂}
	\multicolumn{3}{l}{〒162-0801　東京都新宿区山吹町361}
	\multicolumn{3}{l}{NAN'UN-DO Co., Ltd.}
	\multicolumn{3}{l}{361 Yamabuki-cho, Shinjuku-ku, Tokyo 162-0801, Japan}
	\multicolumn{3}{l}{振替口座：00160-0-46863}
	\multicolumn{3}{l}{TEL: 03-3268-2311（営業部：学校関係）}
	\multicolumn{3}{l}{　　　 03-3268-2384（営業部：書店関係）}
	\multicolumn{3}{l}{　　　 03-3268-2387（編集部）}
	\multicolumn{3}{l}{FAX: 03-3269-2486}
編集者	\multicolumn{3}{l}{加藤　敦}
製　版	\multicolumn{3}{l}{橋本　佳子}
装　丁	\multicolumn{3}{l}{銀月堂}
検　印	\multicolumn{3}{l}{省　略}
コード	\multicolumn{3}{l}{ISBN978-4-523-17874-3　C0082}

Printed in Japan

E-mail　nanundo@post.email.ne.jp
URL　https://www.nanun-do.co.jp/

南雲堂好評新TOEIC対策本！

英語の師匠 **オーガ＆セイン** プレゼンツ

デイビット・セイン／大賀リエ 著

TOEIC® テスト攻略 トントンメソッド

トントン拍子でスコア・アップ！夢をかなえる学習法！

あっ、いいのみつけた!!
TOEIC 400点～600点レベル
（154ページ）

いいねぇ、これだよこれ!!
TOEIC 500点～700点レベル
（154ページ）

特長1 コロコロ覚えるTOEIC頻出英単語！

特長2 ドンドン読めるスピード・リーディング！

特長3 グングンわかるシャドーイング！

おっ、高得点への近道発見!!
TOEIC 600点～800点レベル
（160ページ）

すごい！やればできた!!
TOEIC 700点～
（180ページ）

四六判　各定価（本体1000円＋税）各巻 MP3 CD-ROM付

南雲堂 〒162-0801 東京都新宿区山吹町361　TEL 03-3268-2384 / FAX 03-3260-5425